ANGELS TEN!

Memoirs of a WWII Spitfire pilot

By Richard Gilman

Produced by:

FriesenPress
Suite 300 – 852 Fort Street
Victoria, BC, Canada V8W 1H8

www.friesenpress.com

Distributed to the trade by The Ingram Book Company

Table of Contents

In Memory of 'John' my brother and my oldest
son who each fought a good fight

With grateful acknowledgement:

Heather Gilman
Diana Meyer
Andrew Gilman
Elisabeth Clarke-Gilman

Foreword

On November 24th, 1941, Richard Gilman crashed his disabled Supermarine Spitfire 4B at high speed into a mud bank beside Shoreham Emergency Airport in Sussex, England. He was only nineteen years old. The accident led to several operations, over a year of hospitalization and many more years of recovery. His days as a fighter pilot were over. I now consider this to be very good news. I do not celebrate his pain and suffering; however, I celebrate that he survived his crash. Because he was no longer able to contribute as a fighter pilot in the RAF, he survived the war, married, had a family, and made significant contributions wherever he went. And the huge benefit for me personally was that I had an amazing man for a father.

Richard never talked much about the war as we grew up. Perhaps we, his children, were too young to understand, maybe he was too busy or it was too painful to recall. I cannot be certain if a trip Richard and I took together to visit his crash site in 1963 started a process of wartime recollection, yet I know it had emotional moments for both of us. Then in 2005, my brothers John and Richard Jr., Dad and I travelled to France for a trip through many of the major war sites from both World Wars. We saw the remnants of battle, we learned about the tragedy for all sides, we learned about our Dad, we learned about each other.

The book you are holding is a collection of memoirs. They are some of my Dad's memories of a time of excitement and great pain. They are important because they help me to understand a little more of what war was like, how it felt and how he was changed. They are also important because the survivors of the last World War are dwindling fast and, too soon, there will be no one to remind us that wars are not solutions.

Thanks Dad.

ANDREW P. GILMAN

Preface

The details for this memoir were compiled in my late 80's from records, photographs and memories. Originally these were gathered as a gift for my grandchildren, a sort of picture for them of what war was like. I only recently decided to publish them as a reminder to others whose families still have echoes of loss and suffering in their background.In the early years of the Second World War, the allies were faced with a vast imbalance of all kinds. We struggled with our deficiencies. Our own training was often far from adequate despite the Air Ministry's best efforts.

Fortunately one of the brightest spots was the growing number of Supermarine Spitfires being constructed. This magnificent aeroplane has for long become legendary.

These personal memoirs are not intended, however, to compete in achievement with the biographies of great airmen who had brilliant careers. Many of them survived, or failed to survive, years of harrowing missions. Yet all of us went through the same type of necessary training (for Fighters, Bombers, Reconnaissance, etc.) and that was supposed to fit us for action.

To maintain security we were trained to communicate in code. After take-off we would often assemble rapidly at 10,000 feet over base known as '**Angels Ten**'. We would then receive precise instructions and proceed from there.

A minority of our ranking leaders held the opinion that the war could *actually* be won exclusively by air. One wonders what would have transpired if this idea had developed with increasing and overwhelming force – maybe no Normandy D-Day invasion ?

As a result large numbers of volunteers for all kinds of aircrew were enrolled and shipped from Britain to Canada, a splendid and much more appropriate location than the crowded and embattled little island of Great Britain. A few of us went to Rhodesia (now Zimbabwe), South Africa or even Texas. Because of the desperate need at first for single-seater fighter pilots, a number of recruits were kept in the U.K.

and pushed through our training in nine months. Then we were to be sent to our squadrons.

With boyish enthusiasm, we had thrown ourselves into the successive air and ground courses. The worst fate we contemplated was to *fail* – in any of the eight obligatory subjects...

Our particular segment of RAF trainees, which included many non-U.K. pilots, tackled the programme with necessary speed and cheerful camaraderie. Yet I would have to say, now looking back, parts of our training seem near suicidal.

Those trained for various forms of aerial warfare were numbered in six figures, from the British Commonwealth alone. Those years, so intense and hurried, were more than a training ground for the War; they were an arena for years that lay ahead. We had no choice but to grow up fast and accept the responsibilities that went along with the decisions that we made. Each turn of events in my life led me to other choices which helped to achieve a satisfying career as an educator, a parent, an administrator and with an eagerness to learn from others.

The greatest memory for most veterans exists not so much in the sphere of action as in that special atmosphere of close co-operation and human companionship. Our main achievement, perhaps in the War is that so many of us *survived*. Each day is still a gift and an opportunity – and for that I am enormously thankful.

RICHARD B. GILMAN

1.

The Day I Joined The Air Force
Without Really Trying

May 29/1940

The Second World War started at the beginning of September, 1939 as far as Britain was concerned. I recall we were in church at the time, listening to the sermon from our minister when a black coated official walked up the aisle and handed him a piece of paper right in the middle of one of his sentences. He stopped, read it briefly, held up his hand and declared, "As of eleven a.m. today a state of war exists between Great Britain and the German Republic."

I was seventeen at the time and, like most of the population I suspect, had only a hazy idea of the real political, military or economic situation.

Three events, none of them of any great significance, have vividly stuck in my mind. The first is that, within hours of the announcement, the air raid sirens sounded, and the majority of the population assumed that a deadly air attack was already in progress. We had been hearing constant reports concerning the events on the Continent—devastation and air battles in Poland as a result of the operation of Blitzkrieg, 'Lightning War'. It turned out that this was a false alarm, and it was actually quite a long time before anything approaching the real thing, heralded by those wailing air raid sirens, actually took place in the UK.

Secondly, as soon as darkness fell, there was somewhat of a ghostly atmosphere in every town and village as a result of the blackout. We had been forewarned that not a chink of light was to be visible from the air, and so curtains were drawn, street lights turned out, and all illuminated shop window displays or neon signs extinguished. This created an eerie effect, something that none of us had ever experienced before. I recall cars navigating roads without the benefit of strong beams shining ahead; all motorists had been issued a device, which looked like a black tin can with a baffle horizontal to the level of the road, to be fixed to the headlights of every car. This had a surprisingly efficient effect which made moving vehicles relatively hard to detect, from the air at night.

The third memory is of schoolboys—gleefully being let out of class—given shovels and being required to dig four foot deep zigzag trenches as a protection against air attack. This was long before air raid shelters were provided in any number, so most of the trenches eventually filled with water and collapsed.

At that time the German armies were far away to the east, and so very little seemed to be happening. The newspapers were full of battles that really had very little impact on our day to day lives. World War I had lasted for four years—a sickening battle of trench warfare that swayed one way then another with the loss of millions of men. One defence line after another gave way on both sides. As a result, in the interwar years, the French constructed what they thought was a defence line to end forever any frontal assault—The Maginot Line. This was an astonishing feat of engineering that stretched for hundreds of miles: guns, ditches, tank traps and underneath a honeycomb of living quarters, hospitals, ammunition and food dumps, stocked with everything the French imagined would be needed for an impregnable system of defence. We heard the Germans had built a parallel line on their Western border, and it seemed to most of us that the war in the west at least was going to be somewhat of a stalemate. The press called it the Phoney War.

On our own little family home front, several things happened: my brother Jack—five years my elder—volunteered and was enlisted in the Air Force; my grandfather's business went bankrupt—partly because of the Spanish Civil War, which had ground to a halt—and we therefore had to move house to a cheaper location.

Having had at least a year of warnings and political crises, when the whistle finally was blown, an air of growing excitement and patriotism was powerfully stirring throughout the country. Men of military age began, on a planned timetable, to sign up, mostly for the Army; fewer signed up for the Navy, and fewer still for the Air Force. As the powers that be realized we were not fighting a 1914–1918 enemy, these priorities slowly but surely changed. It was the Air Force that became the main focus, and within the Air Force itself, fighters—for defence—were the immediate priority; offensive bombers only became a focus later on.

Not having a father at home, and being the youngest by far, I received very little advice as to what I should do. Counselling wasn't something that existed in the schools, nor did I receive any advice—that I can recall—from any male relative or friend. In addition I had a poor opinion of myself and was under the impression that most of the people I knew shared this opinion. What was I to do?

Printed daily in the newspapers was a list of the various services, and everyone knew that, eventually, every male and female between the ages of sixteen and sixty would be mobilized, in some capacity, to enlist in organizations that would further the war effort—that is unless they volunteered ahead of time for one of the more dangerous occupations. I spotted an advertisement for messengers, aged seventeen to nineteen, for the Fire Service. I presumed that, since we were going to be bombed out of our heads, this was something I could do; I had a bicycle and no special training seemed to be necessary, so I went down to the fire station and signed up. I do not recall that I was received with either great enthusiasm or very serious purpose in the small town where I lived.

In another attempt to occupy my time constructively I joined the Local Defence Volunteers (LDV) – very soon after re-christened The Home Guard. This was set up by the Government as a new, but necessary, military organization – unqualified and unpaid – mainly composed of older men and boys. It was intended as a back-up for the army in the event of an enemy invasion. After the war the HG was lampooned in a series of popular comedies – 'Dad's Army' – but actually as the threat of German invasion became very serious, its deployment and numbers were not regarded as a joke.

My next attempt at employment—again through information in the press—was for assistance in the YMCA canteens that were to be set up at every military base in the country and overseas. The address to apply was in Liverpool, the large industrial port city on the River Mersey in northwest England, a mere twenty miles away from my home. Accordingly, I walked down to the nearest electric train station without discussing the matter with any members of my family, all of whom seemed to have their own concerns, and in less than an hour I arrived at Exchange Station on the west side of Liverpool. I walked a mile or so up Renshaw Street to the large YMCA headquarters, where I presented myself and was given a form to fill in.

Having just turned eighteen, there wasn't too much that I could say, so I waited until my name was called and handed my form to an elderly individual, who again—as far as I could tell—was neither very interested nor impressed with my application. He talked with me for a time and said there were no immediate openings for canteen assistants. He implied that it wouldn't be long before I would be required to register for the Army anyway, but he took my name and said he would let me know if anything turned up. I found my way through the front doors into the bright sunlight of a Liverpool afternoon with very little idea of what I should do next, so I considered simply returning home.

Facing me across the street, however, was an enormous sign which read: Royal Air Force Recruiting Centre. The words were bracketed by two large red, white, and blue roundels, and in smaller letters underneath were the words: *Why Not Join Now?* Without the slightest intention whatsoever of joining, it seemed to me that, since my brother had already enlisted in the Air Force as aircrew, there would be no harm in finding out a little more about the service.

I walked across the street to where a sergeant in a blue uniform stood outside and addressed me with a measure of cheerful politeness. "Why don't you go in and talk to that bloke sitting behind the table there?"

Inside, the bloke at the table wore a warrant officer's uniform. He looked up as I approached and said, "Sit down." He nodded to a chair, and when I sat down he asked, "Have you thought about applying for aircrew?"

I sat there looking somewhat vacant and nonplussed; I had the impression that anyone who would fly with the Air Force had to be an able, daring, and well-educated individual. Surely, that couldn't be me, could it?

The W.O., pulling a piece of paper towards him, proceeded to ask me a few harmless questions; how old I was, how far I had reached in school, had I had any cadet training, etc. When he was finished, to my surprise, he said quite crisply, "You are just the kind of guy that we need. It will probably be sometime before we have room for you, but why don't you go across the corridor there and talk to that man and see if he thinks you would be able to pass the medical."

Good, I thought, and swept along by a certain air of positivity, I did as he suggested. I was hailed by a white-coated medico who told me to sit down, fired some questions at me, looked in my two ears, two eyes, tapped my chest, scribbled something on a piece of paper and said, "You'll do." I was told to go back to the first bloke in the blue warrant officer's uniform.

I was then requested to sign a form indicating that—if they had room—I would be eligible for further testing and—if satisfactory—pilot training. "The way things are going," he said, "you will probably have quite a long wait, but you might as well sign here anyway for now, and we will be in touch with you."

Still rather bemused, but not unimpressed by his attitude, I signed the paper. "Well then," he said, "raise your right hand." He had me swear a short traditional oath—*I swear by Almighty God that I will be faithful and bear true allegiance to His Majesty King George VI, his heirs and successors and that I will as in duty bound honestly and faithfully defend His Majesty, his heirs and successors in person, crown and dignity against all enemies and will observe and obey all orders of His Majesty, his heirs and successors and of the generals and officers set over me*—and then said cheerily, "So now you are in the Air Force." He shook my hand and indicated the front door. I went out into the sunlight feeling that perhaps someone needed me after all—and with a lot more confidence than when I had left the YMCA or still earlier the Auxiliary Fire Service.

I took the train home, went into the kitchen, and saw my sister, who enquired what I had been doing. I responded "I just joined the Air Force!"

"Oh, you *haven't*." she whispered. I told her that it would probably be a long time before my number would come up anyway, so there was no harm done. That was the end of May 1940; within two weeks I received a letter ordering me to report to an RAF Assessment Centre about forty miles away.

After two days of intensive educational, medical, physiological, and psychological testing, I received a notice that I would shortly be called up for full-time duty and commence pilot training. My intake group were all put through the same tests and out of a hundred approximately twenty-five percent of us were selected as future fighter pilots. The rest were judged to be temperamentally more suitable for bombers, coastal or transport commands, which were equally necessary but likely to be kept waiting longer until the required planes and organizations had been set up for the somewhat later phase of the war.

As for me, I had never flown in my life. Moreover, I had never been inside an aircraft of any kind. Before flying instruction could commence, we all had an intensive course of ground training comprised of eight subjects, all of which required a passing grade of at least eighty percent. There were courses in navigation, meteorology, engines, etc. I arrived for permanent service at Babbacombe, in the County of Devonshire, on August 5th, 1940 and was swept up in a whirlwind of activities at a series of different training stations – until I was deemed qualified.

Tiger Moth. We trained on the DH 82, a rugged little aircraft, at No.11 EFTS (Elementary Flying Training School); stationed at Perth, Scotland, October 1940. Most of us went solo in about 8 hours"

2.

Tough Training For Five Young Comrades

November 1940 to March 1941

For nineteen weeks we were inseparable. I am not sure just why we melded together as a group of five young aircrew trainees but we did. We ate together, shared a barrack hut, flew on the same days, and talked over our problems. With boyish bravado we called ourselves the 'five crazy aces'.

November 13th, 1940 was a thoroughly dismal day as our troop train pulled into Montrose station, a small town midway up the east coast of Scotland. The rain was pelting down in buckets. We had been told the aerodrome was north of the town, so we expected there would be a few RAF trucks lined up to transport us with our kit bags; no such luck however.

We formed up on the platform in *flights*—the equivalent of army platoons. Wisely we had fished out our rain capes, but they did little more than cover the upper part of our uniform. As we stood there, the rain trickled steadily down our necks. It wasn't long before we were soaked through and through.

A fresh-faced young corporal materialized from the station waiting room and announced that he'd be marching us to the base, so off we trudged, kit bags on our shoulders and feeling more dejected by the minute. At least, we told ourselves, there would be a hot meal and a bed at the end of the day. As it turned out, our hopes were a bit too rosy.

As we swung through the gates of No. 8 SFTS (Service Flying Training School) and passed the guardhouse, we figured the first stop would be one of the barrack blocks. We were cold and wet—but instead the corporal marched us to the Sergeants' Mess. The column halted, left-turned, put down its baggage, stood at ease and waited. It was dusk by this time and we could see our corporal, who was also very wet by now, enter the mess and, through the windows, watch him as he went up to a large individual who was holding forth to a group with a large tankard in his hand.

The large individual nodded and continued to chat to his companions. Meanwhile we waited and waited. The rain continued its steady downpour.

A few muttered comments and questions were directed to the corporal, who by this time had come out to join his charges in the rain. It transpired that these were the quarters of the Wing Warrant Officer, the highest ranking non-commissioned officer on the station, and it was his custom to cast a critical eye personally over each new intake. In the Army he would be roughly equivalent to a Regimental Sergeant Major. This was the rank that anyone in the military knew you *never* argued with. He wielded almost total power. Even many of the younger officers never dared to cross him.

It was clear to us the WWO was absolutely in no hurry whatsoever to greet us. He continued to consume his beer, still in full view of our soggy contingent outside. The rain continued steadily. At last having humiliated us with his total disdain, the great man sauntered out, wearing a large waterproof service coat, and we were called to attention. Without a word he walked up and down our ranks from one end to the other. His face was marked by what seemed to be a permanent scowl. Eventually he came to rest in front of us. He spoke very clearly, very deliberately and without a trace of any warmth: "In this unit," he said, "we turn out three kinds of pilots; good'uns, bad'uns, and ones in boxes. So watch out."

At that he curtly turned on his heel and stalked away back to the warmth of his mess. That was our welcome. It was not difficult for us to learn, from practically everyone we met after arrival, that the man was universally hated. As eighteen to twenty-one year-olds we didn't waste much time trying to figure out this character. Whenever we saw him in the next few weeks, he seemed to be still scowling, so we steered clear of his presence. Later on we did a bit of discussing and wondering how any individual could psychologically become such a tyrant. Later still we came up with a few clues.

Montrose was not a happy station. The Germans, a short while before, had carried out a bombing raid on the central part of the facilities. The cookhouse and the central water main had been hit. As a consequence, for quite some time, we had no hot water and perilously little hot food. The facilities for the likes of us Leading Aircraftmen, just one rung up from the very bottom of the ladder, were miserable. There was no cinema, no chapel, no games room that I can recall, and the tea in the canteen tasted strongly of carbolic soap. LACs would sit for mealtimes at the long wood tables. At times we would hear the sound of hobnailed boots and the shouted warning "Mind your plates, please." meant the kitchen orderlies were coming. We would pick up our mess tins and lean well back as they tramped down the centre of the table with a twelve inch broom, sweeping off the crusts left behind by other diners and depositing great clods of mud and snow in front of us in the process.

Our barrack blocks were Nissan huts with small pot-bellied stoves in the centre. Since this was the coldest, snowiest winter for many years, we were generally COLD. We scrounged what bits of coal and wood we could find, and most of us slept in our clothes for much of our stay. Our flying boots, in the morning, were often frozen solid to the floor, and we had to knock 'em off with the fire-irons.

The five of us agreed that the camp was a disgrace and the morale of its personnel was abysmal—a graphic lesson, in leadership or the absence of it.

The Sick Quarters were little better. Anyone who was ill had to report at six am outside and be marched down to the 'hospital' where we waited in a drafty corridor, often for an hour or so, until we were seen by a medical officer. I tried it myself once; I had a temperature of 104 degrees and the MO gave me eight Aspirins and told me to swallow them together. Not surprisingly the thermometer, in a few hours, registered a cool 94 degrees, and I was put on light duties which translated into scrubbing one of the wards. I left as soon as I could, walked back to my barracks, and never reported sick again.

Somehow we got through the course, and by the end of March we were able to buy—Yes, buy!—our own Wings. There was no passing out parade with bands and festivities for us in the UK. We saw our names listed in the official gazette as Pilot Officers, or Sgt. Pilots; and we went off to Operational Training Unit for a month before proceeding to our operational squadrons.

As I recall, a number of the new Pilot Officers, having just passed their final exams and resplendent in brand new commissioned uniforms, just happened by the WWO's office and, of course, according to strict protocol, insisted on a proper salute from the gentleman—now of lower rank—who had so courteously welcomed them in the rain not so very long before.

The Five Crazy Aces...

By far the best part of our time at Montrose was the comradeship that existed between the five of us. So now I would like to introduce you to the members of this small group of ours: Gerry, Roy, Mike, Ross, and myself ('Gilly').

I'll start with young GERRY. He was a tall, fresh-faced lad with a perpetually cheerful disposition and a ready laugh. I never remember him doing anything mean or selfish. He was open and easy to talk to, and we would sit and discuss all our flying problems and difficulties with aerobatics and night flying. I think I was the last one of us to have a conversation with Gerry, just a brief one.

The night was profoundly dark and very cold. Each of us had to do a prescribed number of takeoffs and landings. Alphabetically I was ahead of Gerry so when I had finished my two—in a fashion that would not net me a good mark from the duty officer instructor watching from the ground—Gerry asked me, "What's it like?" He seemed concerned, and I understood why. My flight had scared me rigid, although we didn't generally discuss our fears publicly much. Amongst the five of us we could be quite frank.

I had deliberately shortened my last flight; because of the lack of any visible moon or stars and the feeling of almost total inadequacy after taking off into total blackness.

Lighting needs a bit of explanation: there were no lights permitted in the town of Montrose and no permanent landing aids around the airfield – except one single red light on the control tower and one each on the tops of the hangars. An Aldis Lamp was utilized by the officer on duty when we made our approach, either to signal giving us permission to land (green), or forcing us to go around again if there was traffic on the field, or we were coming in over the boundary too high (red). I was supposed to stooge around the area a bit for night experience before returning, but this I did not do – the weather was too dangerous. As soon as I was up I made a very wide circuit and, like a chicken, then tried to make it the shortest time I could get away with...I told Gerry how I felt and suggested, if he was worried with visibility, he might do the same as I did. Then I headed for my barrack block via the parachute repository.

It seemed I had only just got to sleep when a hand was shaking me awake. I was still in flying kit, cold and far too exhausted to bother shedding it. "There's a crash at the edge of the field," said a voice, "and I think it's Gerry."

We both stumbled out into the cold, and, yes there was a brilliant light about a quarter mile away, the unmistakable fire of a training aircraft with a full tank of gasoline aboard. It must have exploded on impact. Our close friend must have died instantly.

Whenever a trainee was killed, it was the custom for six airmen, usually from the same course, to carry the coffin down to the railway station where it would be loaded onto the guard's van for shipping back to the home of his next of kin. It became quite a usual, solemn routine. A particularly insensitive twist – we were told it was designed by the WWO himself – was the use of the victim's best friends to carry the casket. In contrast with today's ceremonial observances, there was no honour guard, no chaplain, not even a flag. As far as any passers-by were concerned we might just as well have been carrying a box of groceries. We walked the nearly two miles with Gerry, in almost total silence.

Two or three days later, the remaining four of us were on a desultory walk around the perimeter, not far from where Gerry had crashed. Most of the remains of his plane had, of course, been cleared away by the crash crew. Someone said, "There's a soccer ball."

'No, it isn't," sung out another of our group, "It's a helmet. Better pick it up, it'll belong to someone." We ambled over the few yards. It was a helmet alright, covered in mud and blackened. Inside was what remained of Gerry's head.

* * *

ROY was the quiet steady one. He was the shortest of our group and had light red hair. Methodical, hardworking and sensibly cautious, Roy had the ability to see the funny side of a situation, relating it with an infectious laugh that could readily transform itself into a quiet giggle. Because of his solid, dependable qualities, when he graduated, he was posted for further training on two-seater Beaufighters—ideal for night patrols and hunting down enemy bombers.

We kept in close touch after we split up. I was best man at his wedding, and he at mine. I remember him rushing up the aisle of our church with less than two minutes to spare, pausing just long enough to roll his trousers down over his muddy flying boots with maps stuck inside. He had no time to stay for even the rather meagre wartime refreshments. He was due back on patrol over Southern England that very evening.

A gifted pilot, he once took me up for a flip where I could observe the skill with which he survived the war. A bit later on I was present at the christening of his first son, who grew into the image of his father, and eventually—or so I heard—became Postmaster General of far away Burma. After which I lost track of him.

★ ★ ★

Then there was MIKE. The first time I set eyes on this tall, lankily built young man with his shock of unruly hair and a perpetually shy quizzical expression, was on the platform at Exeter station in the Spring of 1940.

I was on my way south to Babbacombe Reception Centre near Torquay. Starting at Liverpool the train picked up several young men in civilian clothes, each clutching a small tightly packed case. It was pretty clear several of us were bound in the same direction.

As the train slid to a stop, I saw a tall couple bidding a fond farewell to their rather embarrassed only son on the platform. They were right outside my carriage window. Little could I have guessed that this was to be my close friend through five different training units, or that ultimately we would end up not only in the same Spitfire fighter squadron, but flying together as partners on operations. That day he certainly did not look like the brilliant and successful Squadron Leader he became. He fought his way through many air battles and came through unscathed.

Eventually he joined the aeronautical industry as a test pilot and adviser, often working with some of the German pilots who had been our sworn enemies in the skies over England and Northwest Europe. Surprisingly we met again, by accident, as old men, in Toronto. At the time both our wives were in very poor health, and to me he looked much the same as his father had looked through that railway carriage window.

★ ★ ★

ROSS, the fourth 'ace', was slightly older than the rest of us. He had been training to be a doctor in a Scottish university, and for reasons I am not sure of—and I suspect he wasn't either—he gave it up to train as a pilot.

We all regarded him as a bit of a brain, and he was probably the best looking of the five of us. He was slow in speech and measured in his movements. He was not a bubbly character, far from it. He was moody and he was also at times prone to absent-mindedness. We all made horrendous mistakes that we happily regaled each other with, like the time Ross took off without his straps properly fastened. When his instructor ordered him to do a slow barrel roll, Ross finished upside down in a heap at the bottom of the cockpit.

He somehow fitted in wonderfully with the rest of us; we were all so different yet made a cheerful team. For Ross, though, life was about to change terribly.

It was another night that I will not forget. The course was nearly over and the next batch of trainees was scheduled to come in and take our place—possibly to be 'welcomed' in the same way that we were.

There were plenty of casualties in action by this time, and there was pressure from the Air Ministry to stick to schedules. The truth was that it was much easier to build aircraft than it was to train pilots. We just had a few more units to complete and then we would be sent on our way. Some of those requirements involved—once again—night flying. The weather in early 1941 had been consistently bad, with the heaviest snowfall Scotland had seen for many years. The order was we were going to fly that night, despite some reported protests, no matter what. Ross and I were both on the list.

I remember my own anxiety, very similar to the night Gerry died; fear graduated to near terror as the night progressed. We had no radio, no navigation aids, and the aerodrome had no proper landing flare path or beacon we could rely on. When taking off we had to steer to the left of a letter T composed of half a dozen goose-necked paraffin flares.

The most prominent feature of Montrose—oft depicted on local postcards—was the large pointed steeple of the church. A short time after I had hesitantly become airborne I became conscious of a rising engine whine and the panicky awareness that my plane was diving despite my efforts to fly it level. I took my eye momentarily off my instruments and looked up—and there was the church tower—*above me!* I was 90 degrees out of my normal horizontal plane. Somehow, in my abysmal inexperience, I righted my training aircraft and missed the Montrose landmark by a hair's breadth. I know I missed it because it's still there and I have it on my screen today.

I concluded my own duty in a clammy sweat, feeling incredibly thankful that my activities for the night were over. As I struggled out of my parachute, Ross came up to me and clutched my arm. His face betrayed how he felt. "What's it like up there?" he whispered—just like Gerry had done a month before.

"Damn awful," I said without equivocation. "Just take off," I urged, "and ignore the instructions to stay aloft to fulfil a time quota. Make a wide circuit and come in as soon as you can."

He gave me an unhappy smile and headed for his plane while I steered for our quarters, feeling totally drained. My next memory was being woken by Roy, I think it was. The time was maybe three am and—*deja vu*—out the window I could see the brilliance of flames once again reflected on the snow. "I think Ross has done what Gerry did." Roy said in a tense, low voice.

The rest of the hut were fast asleep. In that miserable middle-of-the-night daze, we both were out and running fast. This time the ambulance had got there first and the medics were loading Ross in, though it would be truer to say they were loading a blackened side of meat. We knew he was alive because as we jogged behind the vehicle we could clearly hear his screams.

To further compound the tragedy, Ross had been married only the previous month, and his young wife had just come for a brief visit to a nearby B&B. Somehow she got the message and the four of us spent a frantic night of waiting while he was being prepared for proper emergency treatment.

Handsome young Ross survived, but he would never look remotely the same again. He suffered burns to four fifths of his body.

He was shipped down to the legendary East Grinstead Plastic Surgery Hospital, fifty miles south of London. Here a steady stream of grotesquely deformed and disfigured RAF aircrew were skilfully and tenderly treated by the famous plastic surgeon Dr. Archibald McIndoe and his magnificent staff. McIndoe was deeply concerned with not merely the body but the spirit as well. He was one of the great medical figures of World War II. Ross spent, I think, about three years there, and to see him after multiple operations and skin grafts was like often looking at a skull that had cellophane stretched over it. Ross told me, on one visit, that he could never get used to the sound of a stranger's quick intake of breath—caught unawares as they came face to face with such a monstrous sight. Of course, the residents of the town at East Grinstead itself were not only used to the 'Guinea Pig Club' of plastic surgery miracles, but as a community, were part of the cure with their attitude of total acceptance in the pubs, the stores, the movies, the churches, etc.

Slowly Ross regained his love of medicine, but he was, like too many burn victims, a damaged personality. He was also desperately lonely. His beautiful, young wife, after a period of intense strain, sadly divorced him. Who could blame her or him? I still have some of her letters.

Eventually Ross qualified as a fully trained doctor and started his own practice. Thirty years after his accident, I was on a visit to England and called in at the famous hospital, hoping to track down his current address. A helpful receptionist met me at the office, and answered my query. "Oh," she said quietly, "haven't you heard? Dr. Ross shot himself last month."

★ ★ ★

GILLY that was the name my friends knew me by during the war. I was the fifth of our once merry little band. We were perhaps a fairly typical cross-section of young men who were just at the right age—or *wrong* age depending on your perspective—to train and fight in the air, in a small corner of a global war.

I was badly wounded myself, in 1941, returning from an operation covering a commando raid over the English Channel. I spent a long time in hospital but underwent nothing remotely like what Ross suffered. I was wonderfully treated by skilled surgeons. Looking back I feel extremely fortunate and nothing but thankful for all the blessings I have received in my life.

However, as I look at the photograph of the five of us, *the crazy aces* who became close comrades seventy years ago, I am transported back to Montrose. It is with affection, admiration, and not without a tear or two that I salute each and every one of them.

Gerry (killed during training)

"right to left: Mike (highly successful, D.F.C., S/Ldr) Ross (terribly burned; after years in hospital committed suicide) Roy (became a steady, skilful night fighter pilot) Richard ('Gilly' – wounded in action, 1 year in hospital) The five comrades at Montrose, Scotland

The Miles Master, an excellent advanced fighter trainer – but no radio!

This church never knew how close it came to losing its steeple!

Myself, just after receiving my Wings, and promoted to Pilot Officer, (aged 18)

Roy's Night Fighter, Boulton – Paul Defiant

3.

A Crowd Helplessly Watches A Friend
While The Tide Comes In

Jan/1941

I think his name was George, and he figured in one of the most tragic and senseless events I ever witnessed.

I didn't know him personally, but he was on the same station, a different course, training just like we were as fighter pilots...

It seems an odd regulation, but it was prominently displayed and strictly enforced. If one's engine went dead or lost total power and the pilot had no alternative but to make a forced landing, then it was obligatory that he keep his undercarriage (undercart for short) retracted. If however he was near an airfield, and there was a clear enough area, he could attempt a landing with his wheels down. Otherwise, no matter how inviting the open spaces below him might appear, he was not permitted to lower those wheels. His belly landing would do serious damage to the underside of the plane, but if he followed procedure there was a better than average chance that he would be able to survive and walk away from it.

By landing in a level area with wheels down there was every likelihood that those wheels would dig into the soil, sand or rutted surface and become suddenly arrested. If that happened, the aircraft could somersault forwards and finish upside down. This would very likely kill the pilot with the plane bursting into flames, and also probably put paid to the crew if any.

I recall a case where the pilot made a perfect three point landing with a dead engine away from the landing area; the machine came to a stop without a spot of damage and the pilot was promptly court-martialed and, as a result, sentenced.

George—that's what I'll call him—was flying solo in a Miles Master, a very efficient fast monoplane trainer. His engine cut out at about 5,000 feet. It was a clear, sunny day with a lot of aircraft carrying out air exercises in the neighbourhood.

There were many airmen on the ground, and slowly a number of us became conscious of this silent plane gliding in slow circles groundwards. At the same time several of our bright yellow Masters were taking off and landing. There was obviously no room for a safe uncontrolled landing or to clear the local skies by signals or radio messages to make way for him.

It so happened that our base was right beside a long sandy shoreline on the Scottish east coast. There was plenty of room there, and if he had followed procedure a safe forced landing—sometimes referred to in the press as a 'crash landing'—would have been eminently possible; but for whatever reason, George thought otherwise. He saw the lovely uncluttered white beach with the tide out, and maybe he thought he would be a hero and save the plane. He decided to land on the beach with his undercart *down*.

He glided in parallel to the sea and did a beautiful three-point landing. The sand unfortunately was very soft; the wheels instantly dug in, up went his tail and with a loud crunching noise he turned over, smashing the Perspex cockpit and trapping his head in the sand. He was lucky not to break his neck; so there he was upside down and still firmly strapped to his seat with his parachute wedged underneath him.

Several of us, who were not individually engaged or waiting to fly, ran over the low strip of dunes and out onto the flat wet sand.

It was clear he was quite alive and some of his buddies cheered, laughed with him, and even jeered, "How are you going to get out of that lot, George?"

If you can imagine what the position of the plane now was in, you will realize the sharp tail would have been driven straight into the sand like a dagger. More guys appeared, the word spread fast and soon there were probably forty of us spaced out under the tailplane, struggling to lift it high enough to free George.

"Come on fellas, altogether now, one, two, three, lift; again...again..." The tail didn't shift a single centimetre. The suction was far too great. George would have to await a crane.

There was more conversation, with the still inverted trainee, and amongst the good-natured crowd. And then someone gave a shout; "Hey, look, the tide has turned. It's starting to come in."

"Where's that crane? They'd better get a move on."

Unfortunately the maintenance hangars were right on the other side of the airfield. The accident also was not visible from the control tower, so no one in authority apparently knew of the extent of the developing problem.

Two or three of the more responsible members of the group sprinted over the dunes and around the perimeter of the airfield to Station Headquarters, but they couldn't find anyone who knew how to get the heavy equipment rolling. "Find the Duty Officer," someone yelled.

"Where's the Engineer Officer?"

"Try the Mess."

By this time thirty minutes or so had elapsed, and the tide was fast coming in along that beautiful flat sandy beach. There were anxious glances, and then a growing sense of panic set in. More fellows were called over, more shoving and pulling and attempts to lift. "Where the heck is that damn crane?"

But the crane didn't come. Where was it? We didn't realize that no one had been found to give the necessary order. There was no one in charge.

Soon the water was lapping against the bottom—actually the top—of the cockpit. We all gazed in growing horror as our imagination began to think the unthinkable. What if the heavy equipment doesn't get here?

It didn't come. There was no crane. There was still no one who gave any of the necessary orders, and there was simply no policy for dealing with a totally unforeseen emergency.

Strangely, I can't remember George making a sound. Maybe mercifully he had lost consciousness.

We watched the water rise up to his helmet top then over his mouth, his head—his body struggled futilely, twitched a few times. The gentle waves were by this time breaking, up and down, rising and falling over his chest but by then he was quite still, there in the watery landscape. Steadily water engulfed the rest of the yellow fuselage. It was hours and hours before a crane came and the rear of the plane was finally lifted, and the young pilot's limp body unstrapped and carried to a waiting ambulance.

The largely teenage crowd had long since dispersed and gone back to barracks or wherever we were supposed to be; everyone of the group who had watched George die felt so close-up and personal—and so helpless. No mention was made of his death that I can recall. There was no observance on the base. I suppose there was an inquiry, but why would we, at our lowly rank, be told the outcome?

His name appeared eventually in the regular official Casualty List: "George—died on active service." Most of us had received a very poignant lesson—though never discussed openly—according to protocol—on the ingredients of a tragedy and the lack of emergency response procedures.

He was one of many who never graduated or received his coveted wings.

I am still not even sure if his name was George.

4.

Mistaken For A Young Einstein

February 1941

I had finished my flying training assignments for the day. It was raining hard, and I was cold. I didn't relish sitting in a bare flight hut until the rest of my unit had done their quota. The hut was actually a large empty packing case, one in which a steady stream of American Thunderbolt fighters were being shipped to England. Inside were a couple of benches and a telephone. I decided to walk back to our barrack block where at least there might be a lit pot-bellied stove.

Flinging my parachute over my shoulder, I started to trudge around the muddy perimeter of the grass airfield. I was just passing station headquarters when a non-commissioned officer came out and shouted at me. "Hey you there! Your name Gilman?"

"Yes Sarge," I said taken aback.

"Well get over here," the NCO said. "You're next in."

At first I had no idea what he was talking about, and then I remembered that this was the day for commissioning interviews. For the last six months a small proportion of our intake had been wearing white flashes tucked into the front of their forage caps. These were small pieces of flannel about eight inches by four, which indicated, by some mysterious system, that the wearer was 'officer material'. I wasn't so designated, though my brother, still undergoing bomber pilot training, somewhere in the Midlands, was.

We were nearing the end of our nineteen week Service Flying Training School located on a bleak stretch of the East coast of Scotland. For those who earned their wings, there would be one further month of training after that on the particular type of aircraft they would be utilizing in action in their first squadron posting.

Generally two thirds of each new qualifying intake would be designated Sergeant Pilots. The other one third would become commissioned officers with the rank of Pilot Officer. This then was the day of their final interviews in front of a selection board of senior officers.

All the 'white flashes' would have been preparing meticulously for this critical parade and personal interview; trousers pressed, buttons polished, boots shining and many nights of swotting up the answers to possible questions. Not me; I was not even on the list and looked right then the scruffiest trainee in sight. Furthermore, my boots were covered in a goodly layer of mud. "You're next," the NCO barked at me again.

I knew this had obviously been a mistake. I was not even on that clipboard. Why would I ever bother to read that particular notice? I loudly protested that I was not supposed to be there and I knew nothing about it. The NCO took not the slightest notice except to say, "You have two minutes before I march you in."

I was convinced that one look at me would be enough for the interviewing board to dismiss me—literally and figuratively. In a daze I scraped chunks of mud off my flying boots and pulled my sodden trousers over the top of them. I quickly breathed over my dull brass buttons and rubbed them fast with my shirt tail. I combed my hair with my dirty fingernails, straightened my tie without a mirror. Suddenly, my introduction: "Attention, left turn, quick march, halt, right turn, LAC Gilman, 1053093 Sir!"

In front of me was a long table covered in green baize, and behind it sat five formidable looking gentlemen each with a row of medal ribbons, a numbered file and a glass of water in front of him. I stood and gazed at them, feeling very foolish, very confused and looking a real mess.

They silently looked me over, and I could see they were not impressed. The Chief Interviewing Officer opened his file, looked up at me, with what I could only interpret as distaste, and asked me to answer two or three perfunctory questions. I think one of these was, *What is the name of our present King?* The other may have been, *What school did I go to?* I suppose the poor man didn't wish to waste the time of the Board, nor did he want to destroy what little confidence I possessed with too withering a glance.

He turned to the officer at the far end of the table and gave a quick nod, as if to indicate, I suppose, that one of them better ask this bird another question...

Now at this point, I have to insert a vital piece of relevant information; my father was a linguist and a scientist of sorts, but as a result of World War I my parents were separated, and I only saw him infrequently. When I did see him he had the habit of making me learn some historical or literary fact by heart. As I was totally useless in mathematics I gleaned very little from him in this field, however for some reason he insisted I recite the value of the Greek term PI—to eight decimal places—a solitary student fact that stood alone yet it was burned into my brain.

Back to the distinguished officer at the end of the table; he must have thought *I'll ask him one easy one and then maybe a toughie.* He cleared his throat looked me in the eye and said deliberately, "Does the term PI mean anything to you?"

A conditioned reflex clicked in my brain. "Yes sir, 3.14159265."

I could see the austere gentleman was somewhat shaken. Every head in the room smartly shot up. The expression on the Chairman's face changed from disgust to astonishment. They obviously thought I was a young Einstein.

I believe they followed with a few more quite harmless questions; I suppose they had to put something down in those empty boxes. My mundane answers must have seemed almost anticlimactic.

I was marched out. I picked up my parachute and went on my way. I realized the whole thing was a colossal mistake. It had to be.

The kicker was when, next day, the results came out posted on the notice board: my name almost topped the list!

Five weeks later I went on leave and broke my journey in London to pick up a brand new Officer's uniform, wings and all.

Soon I was due to go into battle at the controls of a Spitfire, the finest and fastest plane of that time that any of our Air Forces possessed.

5.

My First (And Nearly Last) Spitfire Solo

April 5, 1941

Of course it *had to be* solo; it was a single-seater fighter. There was no room for an instructor. Once you were strapped into the cockpit you were on your own. This was it.

It was the very last step of our all-too-short training. So now we were supposed to be ready to take the controls and actually fly the bird and then join our operational squadron.

The Spitfire was the fastest, most aerodynamic aircraft manufactured for the RAF early in World War II. It became the acme for defence; likewise for attack. Everyone who flew the Spitfire described it in superlative terms. It is still legendary.

I had arrived at my Operational Training Unit the night before. Fighter pilots were in short supply. The instructors at the OTU lost no time therefore starting in on us. A list was posted: names in alphabetical order and beside each the name of a staff pilot. The general idea was that we would learn firsthand from this expert on the ground. A second list indicated an aircraft number and estimated time of flight or ETF.

Just before my assignment, I called in at the parachute section, signed for my equipment—this particular trade was all staffed by women technicians. Then I went in search of the officer who would be giving me a detailed introduction to my new plane—or so I thought.

I found him in the Mess, and it didn't take long to figure out why he wasn't out on the airfield—and maybe why he was in this unit to begin with.

Pilots left their active squadrons for very specific reasons: they had performed so well, they were promoted—often with a DFC medal on their chest—or granted a much needed leave; they were wounded and headed for hospital; or posted in boxes as it was sometimes known, or just plain KIA.

There were however two more categories. A pilot might have the dreaded LMF letters stamped across his documents. LMF stood for Lacking Moral Fibre—a euphemism, sometimes very unfairly, for cowardice. Finally there were times pilots found themselves so stressed out they were politely referred to by such unofficial labels as 'flak-happy' or badly needing a change.

My Staff Pilot was probably in the latter category, I felt. Not only was he excessively casual, but to put it kindly, he had had a liquid breakfast.

Side by side we headed for the parked aircraft by what I could only describe as a slightly zigzag route. "Hop in," he said to me, indicating the cockpit of the assigned Spitfire, after a certain amount of close scrutiny in front of the quite clearly marked painted number. I donned my parachute, the ground crew strapped me in, and I was then expecting a detailed description of each of the 83 odd instruments, dials and switches before my first takeoff.

By this time my mentor had hauled himself up and was standing on my port wing, hanging on to the left side of my cockpit. "Well," he said nonchalantly, "It's all pretty simple; there's the throttle, the pitch, the flaps, the undercart, the trim; the oxygen's down there somewhere on the left and the radio up top by your hand with the four channels; the gun button's by your right thumb. The Sperry panel with the usual six instruments is all pretty standard, so you're on your own now. Good luck." The last syllable sounded remarkably like a hiccup.

And then he was gone. I opened my mouth to say something, but he was by then halfway to the Mess. I had a flood of questions, but they all died on my lips. They would just have to wait until after my maiden voyage! There was no other knowledgeable individual in sight, and I was too embarrassed to ask either of the two aircraftmen who were patiently waiting for my hand signal. As far as they knew I was a trained pilot—or surely I must be.

A message crackled in my headphones, something to the effect of, "Are you all set to go Pilot Officer Gilman?" I sat there, motionless, for what must have seemed far too long. At last I gave a nod. The engine roared into life and the starter trolley was trundled away.

I waved my hand nervously from side to side. Right away I could feel a slight movement, straining under my hand like a greyhound in check, indicating the two wheel chocks had been pulled away. I was excited, but I had a very tight feeling inside my stomach. I had barely touched the throttle, but the sleek beast promptly moved as if with a mind of its own, and gradually we taxied towards the downwind end of the runway.

A green Aldis lamp from the control tower flashed in my direction. I turned sideways, right angle to the line of takeoff, did my last minute required cockpit check—seven carefully memorized items by the book. There were two more green flashes from the tower, so I aligned my kite with the runway and cautiously opened the throttle.

Well, I thought I opened it cautiously but apparently the 1150 horsepower Merlin engine thought quite differently. My distinct impression was that there was a powerful little man somewhere between my shoulder blades; he kept thumping me harder as I started to push forward the throttle, more and more until it was right up to the gate as I was supposed to do. The idea that I was taking the aircraft off was completely erroneous; it was taking me. There was a slight bounce and then the end of the runway was slipping away under my starboard wing. Before I realized it, I was airborne. I struggled with the control column to keep the speed, the rate of climb and the engine revs where I thought they should be, but I felt almost powerless in the hands of all that horsepower. My nose was pointing up, and I was being pulled higher and higher, faster than I had ever experienced in my last training aircraft.

Eventually I looked at my altimeter and to my shocked surprise, I had already reached 9,000 feet and still had my wheels down! They should have been raised after about 100 feet.

I decided it was time to have done the normal thing for any single-seater operational monoplane, namely to retract my undercarriage. I moved the lever and that was when my real trouble started. It was very nearly the end of my flying career.

There was one specific and very important fact my too vague guide had failed to tell me—or maybe I just hadn't heard that bit of his rapid-fire instruction. It should have not just been mentioned but *emphasized*—a small four-letter word...

The wheels retracted smartly with two nice metallic clicks, and in the same instant the nose shot up several degrees skywards. I struggled with the control column with all my muscle power to force it down, pushing it away from me while at the same time adjusting the trim a good solid turn as I had been taught to do on my very much slower Miles Master—and it seemed to make no difference whatever to the angle. I just couldn't force my control column forward. I knew that if I didn't get that nose down quickly, the aircraft would inevitably stall and go into a spin—by then I would be too low to correct for comfort—and I would crash. I frantically asked myself, what was *wrong*? Perspiration flooded my neck. This was going to be my first and last Spitfire flight. All for the want of a four-letter word.

That word? TRIM.

Yes, the staff pilot had mentioned it to me but he sure didn't underline it! A trim is a structural device fitted to the ailerons, which, when set properly, enables the pilot to fly the plane with such a light touch that two fingers on the column are often enough. I on the other hand was struggling with a writhing python—and the python was winning.

I gave the trim wheel another half turn, without much confidence, just in case it needed a bit more perhaps... there was a very slight improvement. I tried again and there was a little more improvement. It so happened that it required what seemed like *several full turns* before my labouring aircraft obediently assumed a straight and level flight. I just had no conception of how sensitive the adjustment was on a high-speed plane such as a Spit.

It wasn't long before I started to respect, and grow amazed by the Spitfire. I soon understood why pilots said they loved this wonderful aeroplane. Now it was responding to me with docile obedience, even as my speed throttled down smoothly to over 300 mph.

Readers might wonder why the Spitfire was so eulogized, so praised, so regarded with such exaggerated affection? It is hard to imagine just how any machine would become so universally revered, and for so long.

As the months slipped by, I slowly but surely became a part of my lovely craft. It was as if we effortlessly were able to become one unit—like a boy experiencing the first thrill of his new bicycle.

To do it a little justice, after my bad beginning, let me mention very briefly a handful of qualities which together made it unique in design and performance: its power was awesome; merely taking off was a wonder. Its rate of climb was incredible. As the war progressed, of course, modifications were made, and its engine output augmented. Each new major change gave it another number from Spitfire Mark I, IIB to VB to IX or XXV and so on, and on to numbers I never had the chance to sample.

To fly it was always a treat. Its handling was amazingly efficient. At close quarters it could out-turn a Messerschmitt ME 109. It was so delicately responsive that its manoeuvrability in action created an ease and unity between man and technology which melded into a flowing organism. The combination resulted not only in such an incomparable fighting machine, but also indefinably at the same time, a thing of sheer beauty. Any Spitfire pilot would agree.

As I thought about it afterwards, in that first terror-filled solo, I just wished that the little word 'trim' had been properly emphasized to me. I wouldn't have treated with such wonton ignorance so beautiful a creation on our first acquaintance.

Later on, my new Spitfire [ON-T of 124 Squadron] was my own special pride and joy, and that of my two faithful ground crew also. We treated it with enormous care and affection. Whenever I climbed into the cockpit, I was genuinely proud and grateful for the opportunity to be at the controls.

"The beautiful plane"

Landing in Spitfire IIB

Landing in Spitfire VB

11. The instrument panel of a Spitfire.

A Spitfire has about 40 separate instruments. Some are switches, cocks, pumps and lamps which do not need continual attention. But more than 20 are dials, mostly with moving needles that register some vital operation in connection with the flight of the aircraft. Fuel-pressure gauges, radiator and oil temperature thermometers are some of these. Six of the most important are grouped on the central panel: top left is the air-speed indicator, next the artificial horizon, then the rate-of-climb indicator; below that is the turn-and-bank indicator; to the left the directional gyroscope; and left again the height indicator.

Cockpit of single-seater Spitfire

6.

Learning That Discretion Is The Better Part Of Valour

April 8, 1941

An alternative title could be *I Chickened Out*, and I am so very glad I did.

Men particularly often get caught up in daring one another. At an early age, it is usually a fun thing. It may involve a bit of embarrassment or saving face but generally it is harmless.

In youthful years, the stakes are a bit higher. It may involve showing off to peers, or the opposite sex, or worse still a dose of danger. And that danger may be deadly.

It continues to any age – some patent exaggeration; from fish stories to new ears, to the brilliance of grandchildren. There may be an attempt to attain a leadership role in the herd.

When men have time on their hands, when they really don't have enough to do, this is when much of the trouble starts. In times of war the conditions are often ripe for serious rivalries, unnecessary injuries, even tragedy. Far too many events in military records start with bravado and then become cloaked in such phrases as *death by misadventure* or *lack of judgement* etc.

I was aware of several such incidents, or near-incidents, while in the Air Force. It was not uncommon for pilots in training, when they were let loose with a new high powered toy, to give way to the temptation—if given the chance—to show off to the girlfriend or, worse, their family. What a golden opportunity ...*a shallow dive, no, let's make that quite a steep dive, and scream over the top of the farm, the home, even the school. I'll show them I can fly this baby! I can almost knock a chimney off...* The chance to firmly establish one's reputation as a tough customer. I've been in this position myself.

Several not only screamed over the top of the girlfriend's house, they actually hit the house; they furthermore demolished the house, occasionally killing said girlfriend as well as themselves. These things really happen.

My particular temptation was to fly under the local river suspension bridge; a number of us new young trainees had talked about it in the Mess.

I can still feel the pit of my stomach aching, my mouth dry, the perspiration trickling down my body despite my warm flying suit. My problem was just a little different.

There down below me was a suspension bridge, with traffic on it across a river. The day was clear and sunny, and the air was calm. I had practiced how accurately I could fly at low altitude over empty landscapes. I could skilfully maintain a steady height about 50 feet over quite a stretch of flat country. That was the real thrill, for that's when you were fully conscious of real speed.

I'd measured the height of the bridge. I knew there was plenty of room; at the speed I would be travelling—150 yards per second—it would all be over in less than two seconds. I would be down and under that bridge. At that ground speed no one would get my number. When it was done I could look back and feel good. I could brag to myself. I could brag (nonchalantly, of course) to others.

Yes, others had done it—or said they'd done it—so why not me? They'd dared me to do it. *Good to push yourself to do something you're afraid of… it's a test of skill… it's a simple test of guts… remember Screwball Beurling, he did things like that and became famous—for a time…*

We were all new to each other; perhaps several felt the need to establish ourselves. *Just steady nerves is all you need. You can't miss for heaven's sake. You've got a good eight feet above you to the bridge and eight feet below to the water, and if you can't hold it steady for a few brief seconds, what are you doing wearing wings?*

The perspiration was cold and trickling steadily down my neck and my back. My stomach was clenched like a fist.

I was flying at 2,000 feet and there, below me, was the bridge, pulling at me like a magnet. A test of my manhood. Was I not already nearly nineteen? And still I hesitated.

This was the third day I'd had this tussle with myself; back and forth I'd travelled—*Get into position, just right… now for that quick dive down to river level… straighten out, skim along the water, steer directly for the bridge…*

I was a whisper away from a manly exploit, a deed the equal of those others that had—reportedly—gone before me and had more courage than I had. I must be a weakling—*but did they really do it? They probably did. But I didn't see them do it. I have not seen anyone do it.*

Now I was soaked in perspiration. *I can't keep this up. I am not going back for a fourth day of indecision.*

Come on, Man. Now or never!

Then a little voice struggling to be heard—*do you have the right to attempt this? To endanger an aircraft that is needed to fight a war, to waste resources, to kill people on the bridge maybe, to kill myself for that matter*—what about my family?

Now or never, where are your guts?

The little voice: *It sometimes takes guts to say no. Don't be a damned fool! Yes or no?*

At this point I pulled hard on my control column. I went up, not down. The answer was NO. To hell with the dare. I've got a life to live. I never tried to fly under any bridge again—even a big one—unless I was ordered to. I have done some adventurous things – a long time later – knowingly – in the sky, on rivers, on mountains; but as safely as possible.

Over the course of my life there have been folks who probably thought I have made decisions too hurriedly, too impulsively, maybe even selfishly—*I hope not.* Life calls for honest, sober examination of motives, which is not always easy. I can still, however, remember that bridge and dithering above it in my sweaty cramped cockpit. *Yes or no?*

Thank God it was no. That, I like to think, was also part of my growing into manhood.

A UK suspension bridge – similar to the one I chickened out of, fortunately. An RAF pilot was later killed here attempting to fly under it.

7.

Sgt. Jones' Very First And Only Operational Flight

July 31, 1941

I can give myself all sorts of reasons why young nineteen year-old Sgt. Jones died on his very first day with us. Inexperience, pilot error, airplane controls or engine failure—any could be an appropriate possibility, but in my heart I cannot shake the conviction that I bore a distinct measure of responsibility in his tragic death, and right in front of my eyes.

As soon as I landed, I gave my CO full details and followed it up with a written report.

That I was not at any time censored or criticized—since I was in charge of the sortie—was due, I am quite sure, to the wisdom and professionalism of S/Ldr. Duke-Woolley. As a highly skilled and decorated pilot, still just twenty-six years old and a born leader of men, I had enormous admiration and respect for 'The Duke', as he was affectionately known.

As CO he welded his new squadron of neophytes into an effective fighter unit. He could be tough and unequivocal in his judgement of the errors we all made, yet he instinctively knew when harsh or insensitive comments would be capable of destroying the progress or the confidence of his mostly-teenage or early-twenty charges.

On several occasions I could easily have been 'damaged' in my too rapid growth from a young so-called qualified member to hopefully a disciplined and reasonably skilled member of a team. It wasn't until much later in my life that I was able to recognize how strongly he had influenced me for the better. Subsequently, when he was a very senior officer, I hope I was able to convey this to him.

The poem that follows was written in honour of Sgt. Jones many years ago, while the details of his untimely death were still fresh in my mind.

SERGEANT JONES

He came to join his squadron
His total training, from schoolroom
To be-winged Sgt. Pilot,
Had run its ten month course;
And now he was ready;
Fresh faced, eager, dubiously confident
But keen to show he could take his place,
A member of a Spitfire dozen
Newly forming up in Scotland's windswept north.
His task that first morning was to show his mettle,
Scout the area, twinned with another nineteen year-old,
A well tried veteran, survivor of six weeks
So...kitted out in full flying gear, they were on the tarmac;
Camera guns synchronized (live ammunition switched off)
So no hopeful boasts or wishful thinking
Might disguise how he'd bested his fellow adversary.
Take one of the better aircraft, Jones; that one's a bit beaten up –
CO's orders—and stay well above the practice 10,000.
They took off together, north, heading for open Atlantic water;
Ten (oxygen on), fifteen, twenty...still in pair formation.
O.K. to go? We'll peel off right and left—and make sure
Your guns are turned to safe...
For ten minutes they wheeled, soared, dived and climbed,
Manoeuvring up-sun, allowing deflection for speed and angle;
Film running through, whenever a telling shot might register.
Then into a mock dog-fight, each tight-turning
To get inside the one in front; tighter and tighter circles,
Controls juddering, each near a high speed stall;
All reflexes taut, all training followed...
All except that telling altimeter,
Now unnoticed, at barely nine thousand feet...
Perhaps the 'mouse' pulled just too hard
Or jerked back just too sharply
On the now horizontal control column;

Maybe even a frayed elevator cable snapped?
None will ever know
The aircraft in an instant flipped sideways
Into a fluttering spin. No problem, Jones,
Just remember your drill...throttle back, opposite rudder,
Pull stick in, stop the spinning, stick forward,
Ease on the power, hold it there... hold it...
Watch your airspeed, give it time and ease it gently,
Gently, out of the dive. You'll make it with some to spare—just
Was it the ground coming up too fast? the regaining dive too slow?
The control wire unresponsive? Whatever cause, the Spitfire –
Sleek and camouflaged and beautiful –
Flipped, like a viper, into a reverse spin; a dreaded contortion,
Too late by far to correct in time, plunging like a fluttering bird
Closer and closer to the grey waves.
The splash, far below, looked puny, unreal, almost lazy
He was there. He was gone.
Down, down went his partner, in slow circles.
No wreckage, no sign, no scar upon that great expanse;
Only an unmarked watery pit,
Deep, deep in my watery bowels
As I still see his face, just an eager, nervous boy,
That July dawn... his first, and only operational flight
In 1941

Richard Gilman
(Flight Lieutenant, Royal Air Force)

Practice Combat

8.

The Day I Nearly Killed His Majesty The King

August 9, 1941

Looking back it was quite a near thing. Privately, I perspire whenever I think what might have been.

It was all so unexpected. Yet like most near-accidents, the chain of events seemed so routine, so natural, so foreseeable. It all just happened—or almost happened—in the summer of 1941.

The security shrouding World War II events—any war in fact—always makes it difficult to disentangle fact from fiction, the real from the unreal, the truth from the fog of propaganda, excuses or denials. The way it occurred, or the way I believe it occurred, went like this:

King George VI spent six years of his reign conscientiously carrying out a multitude of official functions. Right from the beginning he was a reluctant sovereign (it should have been his older brother Edward VIII). He was not a very strong man—he died in 1952 at the early age of 56—nor was he a very confident or commanding personality. He was, however, affectionately regarded. His presence always seemed to deliver a boost not only in the drab and often much bombed British urban landscape but also among the three armed services he frequently visited in those crowded war years.

Sometimes he was accompanied by his daughter, Elizabeth, the present Queen of Great Britain and Canada.

On one of those occasions he was scheduled to visit the Orkneys, a group of largely barren and windswept islands less than twenty miles to the northeast of Scotland. To get there he would have to cross by sea the choppy, often stormy channel of the Pentland Firth. What he was to inspect, I have forgotten; probably ships of the Scapa Flow naval base. It was the first of his six visits there. Naturally we were not told in advance.

In 1917, as Prince Albert, a very junior officer, he had left the navy—which he apparently hated—and transferred to the new Royal Naval Air Service. It was reported that the King in later life would often have preferred to fly to his rendezvous but the Privy Council and the Chiefs of Staff had decided that travelling by air was, in that early wartime, too risky. The King's younger brother, the Duke of Kent, was killed when his aircraft flew into a northern mountain side only one year later.

In any event, George VI wanted to fly to the island. Just how the decision was reached I have no idea. It was rumoured to be a rare exception to the rule. Much later, in 1943, he went to North Africa by air. Somehow hurried and highly secret arrangements were made to grant him his wish. The King had been whisked to Inverness by train from London, and by early on the following morning a sturdy civilian-type transport plane, specially cleaned up, was ready for him and his party.

As a just minted and vastly inexperienced nineteen year-old Canadian fighter pilot, I had been stationed with our newly formed Spitfire squadron, at the most northern mainland British airbase. Our task there was divided three ways: One, flying out to meet and then help protect vital convoys loaded with arms, ammunition, oil and food, sailing to supply Britain from North America via the route south of Iceland; two, being available to intercept possible enemy raids from their Norwegian bases—incidentally the Focke-Wulf Condors were the largest planes in any air force at that time; and three, rigorous squadron training. This latter was deemed to be vital for our effectiveness—and for our own survival—particularly as we were such new material. We soon would be moving into the busiest operational area of all, south of London and across the Channel towards Nazi occupied France.

Now and again we had specialized unexpected assignments to perform. Such was the case on August 9, 1941. Clearly, from the above we were not exactly selected as an elite outfit. Just a year before most of us had been clerks or students. The air force desperately needed new air crew. For fighter pilots our training was short. At the age of twenty-seven, the commanding officer with his Distinguished Flying Cross was considered by us an old man.

Elements of three nearby Spitfire squadrons were ordered at short notice to escort a VIP. The previous day my own flying records show I was sent to an air base a bit further south to check up on some details.

My log book next states, *Escort the King*. Only later would we officially learn the true identity of our charge.

Before we took off from nearby Kinloss, early briefing had placed our B-flight—6 aircraft—on station closest to the then unknown important personage. We took off on schedule; so did the Royal transport.

Forecasts then were notoriously unreliable. The weather, though summer, was poor right at the start; mist, rain, and heavy clouds above. As the widely spaced escort approached the northern coast, conditions got steadily worse. The view ahead turned to fog, the strong winds increased and as we were fairly low, flying became more bumpy.

In normal circumstances the routine would have been for units to spread out more, separating by altitude and course heading for the sake of safety. On this occasion, escorting protectively a single aircraft as distinct from a group of bombers, it was necessary to do the opposite. We closed up.

The denser the visibility, the nearer we edged towards the VIP. To fly in close formation—like The Snowbirds—even in the best conditions is exhausting. Eventually, I had approached as close as I dared while still managing to keep this slow—rather lumbering but precious—airplane in view. Maybe the whole operation should have been called off, but I suppose the planned ceremonies, the sense of pride and reputations might all have been factors. On we went.

I could now clearly see the passengers through the Perspex windows. Concentrating with all the intensity I could muster, I was making constant minute adjustments to the throttle and control column. Nothing else mattered as I looked only at the adjacent wing, bucking and bouncing to starboard, by this time only a few feet away.

For a brief moment, however, I couldn't help seeing one face I recognized. He was moving the curtains to get a better view of my Spitfire. The uniformed, well-known and bemedalled gentleman seemed to me to be registering a very apprehensive expression. I think his emotions were justified. We were by now in very dangerous flying conditions.

I'm not quite sure how long this continued but, I know that in my cold and unheated cockpit, under my overalls I was soaked with sweat. It wasn't until much later I began to realize what would have occurred had our wings even just touched. There is still today almost never much doubt about the outcome when there is a collision in mid-air.

The welcome order at last came to "break off escort". I wheeled away to port with the immediate next aircraft formating on me. The King's pilot throttled back and slowly descended to what must have been a bit of a rough landing on the target island airfield.

Returning to base, we all landed, parked our planes near the bomb-proof dispersal storage, jumped into our Commer truck and headed thankfully for the mess. Not for long however, as I see from my log that two emergency "scrambles" were ordered later for the same day—because of unidentified aircraft—and I was aloft for a further 2.2 hours.

This little incident was forgotten until recently when I was thumbing through some old files. I sometimes wonder now if it all occurred but there it is in black and white, chapter and verse. It may well be that officialdom, if such records had existed at that time, might have said it never happened like that. It wasn't permitted for the King to fly. His biographers probably never heard of it, and if enquiries had ever been made it would be much easier to deny it completely. Hmmm...

At times I have wondered if the face was that of a double, and the lone aircraft a decoy? Or maybe a colourful creation of a youthful imagination? Yet, as one insignificant young Vancouver-born pilot, I realize that I might very well have changed the course of Royal History—and secured for myself an ignominious reputation.

B Flight 124 Squadron, 1941 L to R: Author, Hornby, Pennington, Day, Turlington?, and mascot. (Missing: Kilburn.)

9.

Dead Radio—Dead Lost!

August 11, 1941

I recall the day I was flying alone, thoroughly lost, on a very dark stormy night, far out at sea and with a dead radio. I really should not have survived. I was still nineteen.

My shift had started at dusk. I'd gone first to the Officers' Mess, had a good but rapid evening meal, taken my carrot pills—to boost my night vision—and called in at the Met Office to check the weather report. Then I went back to my quarters to don an extra layer of woolies under my flying kit and review my own special chosen equipment. I was as ready as I could be. The transport arrived on time, and we headed out for the Spitfire blast-protected area, with our 'chutes over our shoulders.

There should have been nothing special about our night tour of duty. I had expected it would last about eight hours.

We were on maximum readiness, which meant that if our B flight dispersal hut received an emergency phone message from Operations, we had a maximum time to race to our personal Spitfire—parked outside already fuelled, armed and inspected—and be in the air over base usually at about 10,000 feet. The lead pilot would then call up and await further radio orders.

We had planned and practised this regular procedure, from our original time of ten minutes until we had shaved it down to three minutes, or 180 seconds. The squadron prided itself on this emergency takeoff known as a *scramble*.

The weather was 10/10. Low cloud, no moon, no stars, pitch black visibility and cold.

There were two of us, myself and my No. 2 Sergeant Pilot Mike, scheduled as a section. Flying single-seater fighters, we were part of a new squadron, one of a growing number of defence units. Neither our type of aircraft nor its equipment were really suited to night fighting—not even very suitable for routine night patrols. There were no specialized two-seater fighter squadrons available here in Scotland at the time, so we had to be prepared, if enemy aircraft were picked up on radar, to take to the air at night.

By the time we had checked in and signed the usual Form 700 for our aircraft, the weather was turning even nastier. I was not feeling particularly enthusiastic about a rapid launch into the heavens.

On reflection, that sounds much too casual. By today's standards my training had been ridiculously short so I was thoroughly apprehensive about responding to any emergency whatsoever. I prayed that the enemy would stay home and that no gung ho controller far away in his warm, safe sector headquarters would pick this night as a good excuse to test our preparedness for action.

The two of us accepted a cup of cocoa from the telephone operator, grabbed a couple of coarse blankets and a pillow from the shelf and, fully clothed in flying kit, lay down on the bunks to try and catch some sleep. I was No. 1 of our duo so if the call came I might be the first and only one to take off.

It was hard to sleep. It started to blow strongly, and I was conscious of heavy rain starting to pelt down on the thin roof above. I'd had very little operational experience of any kind so far and less than six hours training in darkness on any type of aircraft and *that* was only on good, clear nights. Surely, the call wouldn't come tonight.

I must have dropped off because the shrill sound of the telephone sliced like a knife into my brain and jarred me into instant activity. My feet must have hit the floor on the second ring.

Our operator's voice confirmed my worst fear, "Yes sir, two aircraft angels 10 over base."

Angels 10 over base – that meant Mike and I had to get to 10,000 feet fast. As he was speaking, the operator reached for the Verey pistol on his desk, threw open the window and, in three seconds, a brilliant red smoky arch soared across the nearest portion of the runway. This was a highly necessary but common safety precaution, night or day, warning any aircraft in the vicinity to keep away and discontinue any landing or takeoff. There was no danger whatever of any of the latter on this miserable night!

After the relative warmth of the pilots' flight hut, the cold night air and the lashing rain stung my face like vicious slaps. I immediately swung into my drill, and my faithful ground crew did likewise—two for each of our two aircraft. I had been conscious while I was resting that they might be even more uncomfortable than I was as they had to shelter as close as they could to the planes they were servicing.

The spent red rocket had barely hit the ground before I was halfway to my plane charging awkwardly as fast as I could. My parachute was beside the wing. Art, the fitter, clipped it smartly onto my back. I leapt onto the wing beside the open cockpit. Gord, the rigger, was already on the opposite side and as I slid into my seat, he expertly fastened my safety straps that secured me to the armour plated backrest.

At the sound of the telephone, Art had pressed the button of my electric starter trolley and the sound of the 1100 hp Merlin engine bursting into life shattered the night. Two streams of light blue flames from the exhaust pipes, sixteen in all, licked down both sides of the engine cowling. This distraction from a clear forward vision demonstrated just how unsuitable Spits were for night combat. Sometime later 'flash screens' were fitted as a temporary remedy; till then we were visually compromised.

I waved away the chocks, eased forward the throttle and my Spitfire ONP leapt forward like the greyhound it was. The next twenty seconds were packed with more intense activity, checking a series of levers, switches, gadgets and dials. My parallel tasks were, however, to cram my helmet on, snap on my oxygen mask, switch on my radio, plug in my microphone; clutching my control column between my knees to keep my hands free. I methodically and rapidly went through the standard routine list that we had all been taught and in training had committed to memory in a twelve-step rhyming sequence.

While this was going on, I was moving my rudder fast from side to side (a pilot could not see over a Spitfire's nose until airborne) to taxi the plane to the downwind end of the concrete runway. Not much more than one minute had elapsed since that clarion telephone call.

There was a thin line of flares down the right side of the runway as we lined up tightly in formation. I pushed the throttle fully open, and as the nose dipped level I could just make out a marker light at the far end. Watching the panel dials with one eye, I eased back the stick, and with the familiar surging feel of power at my back, I was quickly airborne and climbing steeply straight into the thick cloud, totally dependent on instruments.

While waiting to break through to a clearer altitude, I had closed the cockpit sliding hood and pushed up my goggles hoping for a better fog-free view. It was the job of my No. 2 to stay on station with me also with the help of our red and green wing lights.

I called up the Sector (who controlled all aircraft once they had left the airbase) and advised them of my presence and altitude. A calm voice gave me a course to steer. This attitude of quiet, confident, unflappability was part of *their* training.

It transpired a Junkers JU88 twin-engine bomber had been picked up and followed on radar flying North along the Scottish coast. We were being vectored towards it and were to be on the lookout to intercept. After a few minutes the 'bandit' turned east across the North Sea apparently heading for Norway, from where it probably had originated. The Air Force had a healthy respect for this excellent and versatile enemy aircraft. I changed course in pursuit, but as reports came in, it was clear the German was faster than us and would probably be streaking towards its base well before I could make contact.

A short while later we that heard two Hurricanes from farther south had intercepted and shot the intruder down into the sea. The cloud was still thick, and we decided to split up so my No. 2 could swing away to port and head for home.

It was at this point my transmission ceased. My radio, on all my four channels, went dead—completely and utterly dead. After urgently trying to coax—or bash—it into action again, I realized, with a slow sense of horror, I was now totally on my own with no visibility and no likely assistance from any source to get me back to base. I briefly began to envy the German pilot who just might have had the chance of a 'fix' on his position for a rescue from the frigid waters of the North Sea. At this point I banished any thoughts of the enemy from my mind. If there had been a whole formation I couldn't have cared less.

Strapped to the right knee most pilots kept a blank compass chart and attached pen. A tiny pencil of light could be directed onto any calculations one could try and make. I drew a rough diagram of the course I thought I had been following, but it was little more than guesswork. I had expected to fly back by compass via radio instructions.

The more I thought about it, the more I realized, given all the circumstances, that my situation was not only desperate, but my survival was becoming increasingly unlikely. There were obviously no lights whatsoever below. There would not have been even if it had been a clear night; the wartime blackout was excellent and strictly enforced.

I tried to think rationally, but it was hard not to give way to a sense of blind panic.

I checked off the possibilities. One, I could climb higher and bail out, hoping I would descend somewhere on land, but it was just as likely I'd hit water somewhere on the way to Scandinavia, where no one would ever look for me.

Two, I could deliberately try and crash-land my aircraft—wheels retracted—using my altimeter to bring me through the cloud at a slower speed and close to the ground. I had a high intensity small searchlight housed in the front of my starboard wing but because of the power involved I could only have the use of it for a limited number of seconds in an emergency; then it would burn out. The chance of finding a clear flat bit of terrain in this soup was a near impossibility, and I could even be flying over mountainous countryside.

Three, I thought of flying further out to sea cautiously and far enough to feel sure that it would be water and not solid rock beneath me. Then, I thought, I would throttle right back and edge towards the Scottish coast diagonally again with my cockpit hood open, goggles down, in the faint hope of spotting the flash of breaking waves along some seashore or even a flat headland.

I had to make up my mind quickly as my fuel would eventually give out, and there was always the possibility I could overshoot Scotland altogether and find myself even more lost in the stormy Atlantic to the west. I was travelling at 300 mph and at over 6000 feet, to be sure I would clear the tops of any mountainous peaks, however, if I was opposite either of the narrow waists of Scotland—each not much more than 50 miles across—it could take me as little as ten minutes to miss this part of the British Isles altogether. I would have to slow down whichever course I took. By now I was functioning, but in a state of numbed resignation; without dwelling on it, I knew that I was finished and a fatal crash would be almost inevitable. Despite my warm clothing, I was soaked in my own sweat. I had to make some decision. Of my three options I decided, with little more than desperation, on No. 3. (This physical condition was not unusual – unless you were a liar).

The chance of actually locating my own base I had long since dismissed—it was just too much of a long shot to contemplate even if the weather had been perfect. At this stage of the war few bases were equipped with circle lights, funnel lights, fog lights—all of which became more and more standard as World War II wore on and the air grew much more 'crowded'. By the end of hostilities the UK was dotted with over 600 airfields. In Northern Scotland in 1941, I am sure they had never even heard of such aids.

The cloud was still thick, and I was flying blindly into an impenetrable wall of dark swirling moisture. I dropped down to a dangerous 200 feet.

Suddenly the blackness ahead of me seemed to grow even blacker and a dizzy spine of granite rock zoomed past my port side. I was heading for huge rocky cliffs—dead ahead. Just in time I jerked my control column back and a succession of jagged black shapes flashed by under my fuselage. I barely cleared the tops of what I later learned were the 800 feet Duncansby Stacks. At least I knew that I was obliquely crossing a coastline now—but where?

Without any more real hope, I thought I had better follow the coast if I could even sense its presence nearby.

It was then that an event occurred that was to me both a total miracle and a literal lifesaver.

Far below me a single feeble light pierced the darkness and I recognized a Morse code call sign of several letters. They repeated just long enough for me to write them on my knee pad.

It was—it had to be—an alert lighthouse keeper who flashed them, an individual whose identity I never knew and regrettably never met. Every lighthouse had a code but for safety's sake did not function in wartime and for obvious reasons. Fortunately I had those codes on my map stuck down the side of my right flying boot and though struggling to fly the plane, still mostly by instruments, I could just pick out the location from where that particular (and wonderful) light came.

The rest is predictable. I was able from that point to steer by map a compass course to base. The sound of my engine eventually alerted the duty pilot at my destination who lit those stupidly beautiful goose-necked paraffin flares beside the runway. I landed, badly I think, but safely. My No. 2 whose radio had not had any problems while landing had already consumed his cocoa and, wondering where I had got to, settled down to some well-earned shuteye.

Back in my quarters eventually I stripped off my flying coveralls. I tossed my soaked underwear on the floor and proceeded to wring out from my blue serge battledress a small basin of perspiration. Crawling over to my bed, I lay down and slept; no dreams, not even exhausted ones. When I awoke, hours later, I knew that I had survived the most terrifying experience, up to that point, of my entire life—and it had absolutely nothing to do with the enemy.

At a later time I read an official report that three quarters of all air force casualties that year were due to non-operational causes—engine failure, pilot error, inexperience, weather, or equipment malfunction. Maybe I almost proved their point.

Duncansby Stacks, NE Scotland (missed by a whisker at night)

Spitfire taking off on a night patrol – not a popular chore

10.

Ordered To Do What Was Strictly Forbidden

August, 1941

I could hardly believe my ears. "You mean I have to go and beat up an armoured column in broad daylight, at ground level?"

"Yep," replied the briefing officer, "knock their blooming aerials off if you like!"

I thought he had to be joking, but this apparently was to be no pointless mission, even though it would be a king-sized thrill for me as a young pilot. Naturally when involved with enemy aircraft there were no air regulations; the only requirement was that we get rid of the enemy—code word bandit or intruder—in any way possible. It was a pretty general regulation that, unless we were taking off, landing or engaged in gunnery exercises, etc., we were to keep above 2000 feet when over our own country. As time went on the ban on low flying was much more strictly enforced.

Of course, many broke the rules, particularly in the early part of World War II. Mix youthful exuberance with the fastest plane the air force possessed and the opportunity to show-off was just too tempting.

Unfortunately, there were several whose names appeared in the regular casualty lists recorded and disguised as KAS or *killed on active service*. When cheap thrills resulted in death—sometimes multiple deaths—it wasn't so cheap. So why was I to be breaking the rules this sunny August morning?

After the debacle at Dunkirk, the Army had been steadily rebuilding. Lessons had been learned from the successes of the German army and Luftwaffe. Camouflage was excellently applied, and a fast-moving pilot needed keen eyes to spot convoys of tanks, guns and supply trucks travelling across the countryside.

The Army, accordingly, had requested the services of some of our fighters to cruise around and stage mock attacks so that the lookouts could obtain experience not only with defensive anti-aircraft fire but also methods of warning the whole column for whatever evasive action might be possible. It was to be a cat and mouse game—and to us, mostly nineteen and twenty year-olds, it sounded like *fun*. I remember, on the first of several individual sorties, I flew around the area noted on my map about fifty miles square where the quarry would be on manoeuvres. With the sun reflecting occasionally on windshields and the evenly-spread columns looking like a line of slugs winding their way through a kitchen garden, we would plan our attack.

Now if you've never tried this *sport* before, you should know that it is not difficult to locate an aircraft in a clear sky because of the noise of its engine; the sound of the enemy planes could usually be distinguished from our own. But there was an exception. If the plane approached from exactly dead ahead or dead astern, travelling fast and low, it was virtually impossible to hear it at all until it was, briefly, right overhead. The troops would, of course, have been told this, but few new recruits would believe it.

At a rough calculation, a plane travelling at 300 mph. was covering 150 yards or 450 feet per second.

For this exercise we would therefore be moving easily at 450 fps and low, and from dead astern. I figured that I would circle around behind any low hills or forest area. We had also been training to do our part one day too! Each of us stalked a column, like a fox in the tall grass around a chicken farm, and then using whatever cover we could, we would pounce.

It is worth pointing out that the higher one flies the less sensation of speed there is. Conversely, at 100 feet or less, everything flashes by in an instant. The thrill factor, unless there is an enemy fighter on one's tail, is absolutely mind-blowing. It's also highly dangerous; tall chimneys, high tension wires, suspension bridges and the like are deadly and claimed many lives on both sides when in action.

I will never forget the first column I *attacked*: all the lookouts were facing away from us, their guns seemed to be pointing straight ahead of the column. As the fox, I wasn't creeping; I screamed over the top of the column. I may have knocked off some of the slender radio aerials, festooned with the regimental coloured pennants.

If anyone had a bad heart, I pitied them because some of us had been strafed on the ground by enemy aircraft ourselves.

These were young troops in training, and I knew what a shattering experience it probably was for them—their first time perhaps. To better the experience, I pumped my left and right rudder slightly simulating the sweep of a hail of .303 ammunition from eight wing machine guns, each firing twenty bullets a second.

Yes, it was a thrill for me. I loved every moment of it, and I can still relive the whole episode even writing this now at age 88, just as if it occurred last week. In the grim reality of warfare, not surprisingly at such times, we felt just little more than boys.

I like to think a few of those soldiers as a result were better trained and more alert when they landed on the Normandy beaches and fought their way inland over the fields of France.

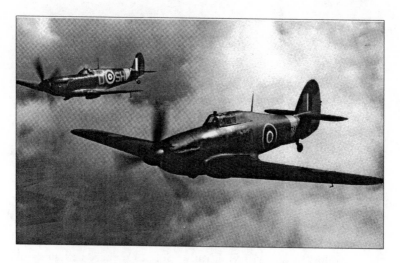

Low Flying. Returning across the Channel from France
(painting by Peter Newton by permission)

11

Bringing My Older Brother Home From The War

August 20, 1941

"Call for Flying Officer Gilman," shouted one of the waiters, trying to make his voice heard above the general buzz of pilot conversation in the crowded Mess. I made my way to the telephone on the end of the bar. In order to get the message, I had to get the caller to repeat it three times.

The caller turned out to be my sister, speaking on a poor line four hundred miles to the south. "Jack was killed last night," she said, with a remarkable degree of control and gentleness in her voice. "He had been returning from a raid over Germany."

With World War II in full swing, we were living, worldwide, in an atmosphere of constant casualties; one could sadly almost get used to the tragic loss of human life. When it came to military colleagues or friends in the same unit, it was a different story. At this stage in northwest Europe, it was the Air Force which suffered the most pronounced death toll. Each aircrew found their own personal way of handling the sudden heart-stopping shock that alternately stunned the mind or chilled the spirit, but we were never expected to show it.

I personally adopted the practice, when learning extreme news, of hearing it but not allowing it to be taken in. I would only absorb it very slowly. I thought of it as my emotional buffer, and it stood me in good stead.

So it was with the news of my brother Jack, five years my senior but also my boyhood hero and best friend. I was nineteen at the time.

My response, I think, must have sounded almost brusque. How could I express any real feeling in the hubbub around me? I simply said I'd call his squadron, get details and obtain permission to fly down hopefully to where his crash occurred. If it was physically possible, I'd arrange to have his body shipped home for a family funeral.

I pushed my way through the noisy crowd to where my commanding officer stood. In three sentences I made my request. Although our squadron was on operations, the Squadron Leader didn't pause for an instant. "Fly down, and do what you can," he said.

The CO was a leader whom I enormously respected as did all the other pilots. There were no fulsome condolences or questions of where I was going or how long I'd be away. I was just about through the door when he called after me. "Gilly, don't take your own plane. Get the maintenance to give you an old one."

A smile and a wave from him and I was away. I nearly stopped for a moment to protest; my plane was new and in top condition. I hated the thought of anyone else tampering with my personal Spitfire, but it had to be left available. The CO, of course, was quite right.

We had no room for personal luggage in a single-seater fighter, except for PJ's which we sometimes tied around the cables of our radio storage compartment. As soon as I had called the Adjutant of Jack's No. 51 Bomber Squadron at Dishforth in Yorkshire, I signed out a beaten up plane from the repair hangar, picked up my parachute and was airborne and heading South in under an hour.

I knew I would have to refuel somewhere, so decided to stop off and grab a quick meal at Drem, the airfield for Edinburgh. My arrival there, as it turned out, was not classic.

I am not sure what happened. Perhaps I was distracted or the undercarriage had suffered damage to one of its oleo legs or the surface was rougher than I thought; I don't know, but as soon as I touched down the left side collapsed, the wing dug in and I cartwheeled to a very undignified stop.

The blood wagon, with its bell ringing, soon hove in sight, and a cheeky young cockney fireman leaned out of his cab, saw me already untangling my pyjamas from the now defunct radio and asked if this was the way I usually arrived for a visit to the Scottish capital.

I apologized to Flying Control, gave my name and number, told them the reason for my trip and headed for the main gate. It would now be hitch-hiking for me the rest of the way. There was no wheeled transport available, and I had virtually no money on me.

I left the remains of my Spitfire in the middle of the airfield, and I don't remember ever hearing of it again nor did questions about it ever pursue me.

Many hours later, after a variety of helpful motorists and truck drivers, I was standing beside a field of vegetables a short distance east of the village of Diss in the County of Norfolk, blackened by the fiery crash of my brother's Whitley. From phone calls to his base, conversations with the County Police and with hospitality from the local Vicar I managed to piece together a rough scenario of what probably had happened.

The bomber had a crew of five; Jack was flying as the co-pilot. It was only his fourth trip over Germany; each one had been fraught with dangerous events and generally inconclusive results. On the night of August 18th, sixty-two aircraft were scheduled to attack the rail yards at Cologne just south of the Rhine. Six aircraft were lost in the raid, five of them Whitleys. Several fires were reported over the target area, but subsequent reports indicated very little damage was actually done since a decoy fire, set by the enemy, had attracted most of the bombs.

Jack's aircraft crashed in flames shortly after reaching the English coast, killing all the crew instantly. A serious fire in the radio compartment had likely spread, but on visiting the 51 Squadron Base, I learned that enemy night fighters had also been active during their return trip. It was possible his burning bomber was an easy target for a German to follow; one of its engines was seen to blow up *before* impact.

The next day I called at his bomber unit in Yorkshire, where I picked up some of his possessions and talked to members of his Squadron. Then I wended my way back to the family home at Southport, in Lancashire.

When the train from the south eventually pulled into the Chapel Street Station and the passengers had all alighted, I was on the platform. Jack's casket was unloaded, draped in a Union Jack, and taken to the local mortuary. The funeral was held in our Anglican Church the next day and his body transported from there to the cemetery grave at nearby Birkdale, where four family members had already been commemorated.

I wish I could say that I remembered all the details of the service or the necessary official activities that followed, but in actual fact I recall very little. I felt that, still being in uniform, I was *on duty*; inside I could only describe my feelings as an invading numbness. I kept my eyes and my thoughts looking straight ahead.

In three days I left for my base. Twenty-four hours later I took my place on a Squadron operation, and two days after that I had my second of three Spitfire crashes and narrowly missed breaking my neck; another pilot did exactly the same thing, but in his case with fatal results.

Now a word about what was really going on within me. It took some time—years in fact—to recognize fully what my brother had meant to me.

He was a truly fine young man. Although only twenty-four, his example and sterling qualities I was increasingly able to cherish.

This is not the place to write his all-too-short biography, but there has to be some meat on the bones of his memory. At five, I was shuttled into his room—to me an enormous promotion! As boys do, we talked together after 'lights out' far into the night. We ping-ponged in the basement with enormous energy and enthusiasm. We golfed for free on the endless local beach of pure sand. We camped in the wild beauty of the Lake District—now a National Park—beside a freezing mountain stream at the foot of one of the fells. Our bacon and eggs never tasted so good as after a bracing morning swim.

Jack became a very junior clerk at Price Waterhouse, Accountants (also for the Oscar Awards) with no more equipment than a sharp pencil and a hard stool. He hated it. When the war started, he declared that it could not be fought from behind a desk, and he enthusiastically was off to join up as a volunteer, training first as a navigator and then as a pilot.

Not too long after, I caught up with him because fighter aircraft, then, were more in demand than bombers. He loved the training, and whenever we met up, he had a spring in his step. He put on weight and never looked healthier. He used to brood however on what the effect was after the bombs were dropped on the German civilians below.

Our joint long-range aim was to return to Canada, the land of our birth; our home had been in Vancouver until our father had gone totally bankrupt as a result of World War I. After the end of this War we were going to work our way across the Continent for free—supposedly by jumping a train. We had it all figured out.

In character, Jack was completely dependable, and he displayed a high sense of responsibility. Every cent of his meagre clerk's salary was allotted in priority: first his church collection, next his board and lodging to our Mother, his commuting train fare, a small allowance to our sister who was not able to earn a wage; what was left over was for his lunches were occasionally almost nonexistent.

At the time of his death, he was engaged to Kay—a beautiful young lady, artistic and talented, who was totally devastated by his death. In some ways she never quite got over the event of his fiery crash.

Some time later, after I was wounded and spent a year in hospital, Kay and I were married, and together brought up four wonderful children. I feel this greatest of blessings has somehow been a legacy from Jack.

His memory remains as fresh today as it ever was.

It would have been so fitting for Jack also to have lived once again on the shores of English Bay, overlooking Vancouver's famous Stanley Park.

As I write these words from my condo on Vancouver Island, it is a strange turn of destiny that it is almost possible to see the very home on the shore of Jericho Beach, across Georgia Strait, where both of us were born.

RAF Whitley, early war heavy bomber (top speed loaded approximately 95 m.p.h.)

My brother Jack, aged 25, crashed in flames
returning from a raid over Cologne

12.

Doing A Somersault With My New Spitfire

August 29, 1941

Northern Scotland is a bright and breezy place. Weather can change as fast as a set of traffic lights.

As the Second World War progressed, more and more airfields were constructed. The locations were decided by a strategy committee—leaving the fine details to a specialized survey body.

The members of this second group were a mixture of professionals: geologists, arborists, soil scientists, meteorologists, together with local experts in agriculture, land use, ownership and transportation patterns. The committees worked together with remarkable speed, co-operation and a surprising lack of bureaucratic roadblocks. The deadline they worked under, and the pressure inherent, generally provided a quite remarkable steady flow of large new red dots—representing airfields—that appeared on the geographical aerial maps which we pilots or navigators stuffed into the top of our flying boots before we took off on an operation.

Given the relative size of the little island known as Great Britain, as the skies became more and more crowded, some of the new airfields grew up very close to one another. Their circuits were represented by the imaginary one way tracks of all the incoming or outgoing air traffic. These circuits, at times, almost overlapped. By the end of the war there were over six hundred local aerial highways.

The base I was posted to was designated as suitable to start up a new fighter squadron. Almost simultaneously a half-dozen brand new Spitfires were flown in by members of the ATA (Air Transport

Auxiliary), many of them young women—and to the surprised ground crew, remarkably good-looking ones at that! A dozen older planes of questionable vintage dribbled in until we had the required complement.

Within a few days a complete ground staff—all strangers to each other—appeared. Several nearby box cars from the nearest rail station disgorged a variety of stores into some waiting trucks en route to the new base. A couple of military police materialized, with distinctive white belts, red hat bands. A Station Headquarters notice was posted near a gleaming white flagpole beside the Main Gate— in fact the *only* gate. Simultaneously concrete was being poured as the metal sheets were arriving for the necessary prefabricated maintenance hangars. Bit by bit the usual trappings of a standard airfield were constructed: mess halls, sick quarters, MET. Office NAFFI canteen—it soon looked as if it had been in commission for years—a bit like one of a chain of new coffee shops. The climate wallahs were quite aware that much of lowland Scotland was of doubtful consistency. After the first require-ment of a suitable level space with sufficient room for taking off at least in two directions and preferably a third one, it was necessary to lay out a tarmac runway that would conform mainly to the prevailing wind. Before this it would be just grass or strong wire mesh (as was later used in Normandy).

Unfortunately in many areas on either side of the runways there was little more than rather squishy bog. When we took off in a hurry we stuck to the safest wind direction possible but in stiffer breezes we had to struggle to avoid any crosswinds blowing us sideways. If taking off was often tough then landing was decidedly much more tricky, particu-larly if the pattern was strongly at nearly right angles. A light plane, as compared to a loaded bomber, would be at a serious disadvantage.

On the 29th August, 1941 I took off for an assignment on my own, and while airborne the wind had veered sharply with gusts of wind at gale force. As I entered the circuit on return I could see the windsocks standing out stiffly horizontal. My gas was getting low. I could perhaps have tried a safe wheels-up landing in a space outside the designated runway but the plane would be automatically badly damaged. I decided to risk it by coming in faster than usual, at about 90 mph airspeed and fly it right down onto the runway, tail up, with no attempt at putting it down on a 3 point touchdown.

Nothing else was flying, so I did a dummy approach first; then I went round again and despite a lot of turbulence I thought I would be able to make it with the undercarriage deployed.

As I crossed the airfield boundary, I could feel the buffeting of the wind gusts. I opened my cockpit, as was usual on the crosswind approach, pushed my goggles up, lowered my flaps and, with my left hand firmly on the throttle, awaited the first contact with the windy runway. My wheels hit the deck rather hard, bounced, bounced again, each time a bit nearer to the side of the runway. I cautiously pumped the brakes, for I had to avoid at all costs a skid or a pitch forward. I was nearing the side of the runway and the soaked and soggy grass just outside the tarmac. It was continuing to drift to my left and I realized I wasn't going to be able to hold it much longer. By this time I was past the point of no return. I didn't have enough room to open up and push the throttle wide open in an attempt to go around again, nor did I have time to imagine who would be watching and wondering if my light Spitfire would be able to stay upright with the rudder and the control column. I knew, with increasing alarm, I was losing.

My wheels crossed the edge of the concrete and I hoped they would still be able to rotate on the so-called grass—but no, I could immediately feel the mud beginning to claw at the tires and grip them in a vice. My engine being the heaviest part of the plane continued forward and down, pulling the tail up. I had a sickening, impotent feeling as if I was about to go over a precipice. Actually I was half way through a rapid somersault. Remember I was going from probably 85 mph to zero in about five seconds.

I could feel the straps biting into my shoulder and paradoxically I was suspended motionless for an instant and then in apparent slow motion I completed the arc, with a shattering of glass my windshield and Perspex buried itself in the soft glue-like mud.

With my neck bent forward, my head was driven downward. As soon as the whirling airscrew hit the ground the steel blades bent backwards and, digging into the greasy soil, stopped the engine.

For a few seconds there was an eerie silence. My legs sticking up in the air and my head buried deep enough for my goggles to be squeezed into a brown soup where I could see nothing.

My first thought was that I might burst into flames and there would likely be no one near enough to help. Despite the wind, I could hear a slow, distinct drip... drip... drip... which brought a panicked wave of fear. I hoped no one would approach smoking a cigarette. Nothing happened, and I was still caught rigidly as in a straight jacket.

Then sounds, still very muffled, seemed to penetrate through my helmet: the siren on the crash wagon, urgent voices, the sound of people scraping attempting first to scoop away lumps of clay and the jagged shards of the cockpit Perspex. From upside down, I caught sight of two bare, bleeding hands trying to dig me out. In no time flat there must have been twenty men there vainly trying to lift my tail, which was sunk deep into the muck like a giant dagger; it was quite useless. The suction would only yield to a large crane – just as I had observed elsewhere as a spectator.

My roommate and fellow pilot, 'Timber' Woods, an ex-Mountie, was the owner of those frantic, bloody hands. Others joined him and eventually enough was dug away for them to support my body and then undo the straps; this was done with great care or the weight above my head could very likely have snapped my already twisted neck.

They eased me out of the sort of tunnel created, and I heard the calm voice of my highly respected CO: "Hop in Gilly," he said to me. I was really shaken up and probably trembling a bit in the Squadron Leader's jeep. I relaxed slightly, thinking to myself, I'll be given a hot cup of cocoa in the Officers' Mess—but no such luck.

The CO was heading for the MO and Sick Quarters. Heck, I only I wanted a bed, so why here? But the CO knew better. "Give him the usual," he said to the MO or words to that effect. Doc Lilley, who was one of the cheeriest guys on the whole Squadron, gave me a glass of water and three or four coloured pills. In five minutes I was back in the Squadron Ldr.'s vehicle and now, surely, to the Mess—wrong again. The CO headed for the aircraft dispersal area. "Flight Sgt.," he crisply barked out to the flight maintenance head, "get a spare kite ready for F/O Gilman. Right away."

"But Sir," I stuttered, "I'm not going up now."

"Yes, you are. Right away!"

He stood there, unsmiling, while I was hosed down by one of the riggers. Feeling distinctly second-hand, I crawled, sore and grumbling under my breath, into the new cockpit. I think I hated him at that moment.

Fortunately the wind had subsided quite a bit. I taxied out very slowly, very deliberately, and I did my cockpit drill very carefully. I turned into the wind and pushed the throttle right open, perspiring in a way that I knew was out of character. I took off still trembling a little, but somehow things settled down as I flew around the area for a few minutes. Then I headed back to base.

I landed very cautiously—and not too bad a landing at that—and wheeled into my usual flight parking spot. I couldn't see the CO, but I knew he'd be watching, somewhere. It wasn't too long before I got my steaming hot mug. There was no namby-pamby, no applause, no *well done, young fella*. I don't recall anyone mentioning it again. But I did notice Timber's bandaged hands, and I nodded to him in a way I knew he got the message.

The whole episode was just another reason that I came to admire S/Ldr Duke-Wooley's leadership so much. He was a far, far wiser man than me! He knew that if I didn't go up at once, I might not ever do so again (as some pilots I learned had found reasons to refuse permanently).

Sometime later, at another nearby Spitfire base, I heard that another pilot, about three inches taller than me, had done exactly the same thing and that the mud crushed his neck so that it broke like a twig. He did not survive.

It was just another day with our squadron, but I learned some valuable lessons as a result. Also it was the second of four crashes I experienced in my Air Force career.

Landing in a gale

13.

Engine Failure, Far Out In The Atlantic

September, 1941

Powerful waves were pounding on the cliffs of a lonely beach just beneath me. I was flying straight towards one of the wildest stretches of coast in the northwest of Scotland at a height of about 800 feet.

My single-seater aircraft was functioning beautifully; my partner's was not. A few hundred feet above sea level he was gliding in silently with a dead engine straight towards those cliffs. At the edge, where the ocean met the shore there was a narrow strip of bare white sand. He was much too low to be able to use his parachute. Whichever way you looked at it there was going to be a crash at any moment—probably a fatal one...

Mike and I had taken off before first light on a cloudy, grey day heading due West. Our orders were to intercept a convoy of about sixty merchant ships sailing from Halifax bound for Glasgow, loaded with food, oil, equipment and ammunition—all supplies vital to the war effort in 1941. Relays were required to keep them under surveillance as they neared the British Isles.

Convoys such as this, under the command of a Naval Commodore, regularly made their way across the North Atlantic, zigzagging erratically to escape the packs of U-boats that increasingly infested the hazardous shipping lanes.

Our compasses were set at 270 degrees somewhere in the direction of the Faroe Islands which lie southeast of Iceland. We only had an approximate location from Naval Intelligence and there was no way we could call up for more accurate information. Strict radio silence was enforced.

It was customary for ships to be assembled in evenly spaced parallel lines covering twenty miles or so of ocean. It was surprising how sixty ships could be so invisible. Camouflage paint and the grey-green Atlantic rollers were together incredibly effective.

We had located the convoy safely, despite the occasional burst of machine gun fire from some overzealous, frightened deckhand. We patrolled up one side, down the other, throttled back for minimum speed, at mast height from end to end; our canopies open, goggles up, a friendly wave now and again. We kept one eye on the sky—a very long range Focke-Wulf might briefly arrive all the way from Norway—the other eye on the surrounding waters where a conning tower might appear or even a pencil-like periscope.

Our fuel gauges indicated that the mission was over. We glanced at our watches to record the time, snapped our hoods closed with the locking device, opened our throttles, zoomed up to a less bumpy 10,000 feet and set our course for home.

A few minutes later, to my surprise, my partner's nose suddenly dropped, and his speed faltered. More hand signals and it was clear he would be forced to ditch. I couldn't make a radio call for help, and bailing out for him in such a watery landscape would have been near suicide. I hovered near him as he steadily lost height, finding it quite difficult to slow my speed and course so that I would not overshoot him and lose sight.

There have been several modern examples of commercial aircraft running out of fuel or experiencing malfunctions over the ocean. Some made it, with a very shallow glide to a nearby airport or some deserted flat or shallow area where a wheels-up landing was possible.

As my partner neared the mist-shrouded coast of the North-west British Isles it was increasingly difficult to keep him in view at all since the upper part of our planes were camouflaged for over-water flying. I wondered if he was going to make land at all and even then what would he do. The visibility was desperately poor. At the altitude I was now flying it was possible to get a sense of the power and height of the huge grey Atlantic rollers just below me.

It seemed to me that Mike was barely skimming the tops of the waves, with his windshield probably drenched in spray. Then I saw there were those massive cliffs dead ahead. With a burst of power I knew I would be able to clear them but it was clearly impossible for my partner to do the same – with a dead engine. At the very base of the cliffs there was a narrow strip of white sand which he must have suddenly seen in the last few seconds, as disaster loomed over his aircraft nose.

With consummate flying skill he just made the edge of that tiny strip at absolute minimum speed – but even then his airspeed, I estimated, had to be close to 100 m.p.h.

Then at the last moment, he jerked the control column back, producing a sudden stall; at the same time he kicked his rudder hard left and allowed his port wing tip to dig into the sand. He cartwheeled to a stop parallel to the cliff face. The manoeuvre was magnificent, and I doubt it could ever be duplicated under such circumstances.

I circled overhead. He hopped out, giving me a wave so I knew he was alright.

I flew back to base – still full of admiration for Mike's exploit – collected some warm clothing, a few tools, food and survival gear, attaching the lot to a small parachute. Light was failing by then, but I thought I could just maybe make it back to the crash site.

Unfortunately there was another problem; my way was blocked by a massive anvil-shaped thundercloud towering up to 18,000 feet, dense to its core. I should have wisely taken the time to circle around it, but I just had none to spare. In my inexperience I did what no pilot should ever do, I plunged forward straight into it, hoping to come out the other side.

My Spitfire was tossed about like a cork in a steaming cauldron. Water vapour seemed to pour into my cockpit from every direction. All my instruments went completely haywire. It would take a detailed page to describe what that turbulent black cloud did to me. It certainly was not a part of my training! Eventually the monster tossed me out on my ear—and quite near ground level too.

I cautiously approached the little beach. So I then knew he was alright. In the dim twilight where my friend had force landed. On the sand beside the crashed Spitfire he had written in driftwood: GONE INLAND, and a large arrow beside it. I dropped my package and returned to base. The next day I was back again; even though it was still the UK, the area was as barren as the Arctic. It actually took two and a half days to get my partner back to the squadron and we even had to get a Navy patrol boat to make a special trip, through Stornoway in the Hebrides, to rescue him from the beach.

I don't know whatever happened to the crumpled wreckage. Personally I wished it could have remained there as a monument to some of the most brilliant flying I ever saw.

14.

A Rudely Interrupted Soccer Match
& Other Strange Goings-On

November 10, 1941

The amazed soccer players suddenly came to a halt and stood rooted to the spot. About five hundred yards away the German planes swept down on the airfield, machine gunning—completely unopposed. There was no warning, and the raid took place with lightning speed...

There was precious little time for sports, for the pilots of RAF Fighter Squadrons in 1941. When in action in the heaviest aerial engagements of the southeast of England around the London area, there was practically none.

Stationed progressively further to the north at airfields in Britain, a little more took place. Occasionally it was felt to be a matter of keeping the aircrews physically fit and for a brief time getting their minds off combat and operational missions.

Our squadron up in the north of Scotland had never even considered a team game. We had been kept just too busy. Someone must have suggested a friendly match between the Spitfire pilots and Station Headquarters. The idea caught on, and one bright breezy afternoon everything came together.

So there we were, decked out in borrowed boots, shin pads and coloured shirts on a rough patch of level ground ready to do battle with a soccer ball. We could have been taken for a cheery bunch of schoolboys.

I can't recall if we'd had official permission, but if we didn't have it, we were certainly breaking the rules. It was mandatory that at least one section always be on instant readiness, but for whatever reason, on that day it was not the case.

The attack was over almost as soon as it had begun.

The pilots were still dressed, with the spectators, in an assortment of anything other than official gear. After those brief frozen moments, the players raced headlong towards the airfield. Minutes before they reached the crew dispersal huts, the enemy were streaking home across the North Sea to their bases in Norway.

Feelings of anger, embarrassment and rotten luck struggled to the surface. There were arguments, disagreements and frustration. Who organized the game anyway, and why were there no radar alerts? There had never been a raid of this kind in this region before—and in broad daylight no less.

It wasn't long before someone uttered the word *sabotage*.

It had been a dark spectre ever since the ignominious 1940 defeat of the fledgling British Expeditionary Force in France, when the remains of the Army in full retreat to the coast were squeezed into the port of Dunkirk. Unceremoniously—yet dramatically—they had largely been able to escape across the Channel from the pursuing Germans. No one knew just who had piled into that disorganized but brave flotilla of little boats and somehow made it back to the shores of the south of England—often with little more than their underwear. It was recognized some 'undesirables' might have been included.

The Germans already had considerable practice in infiltrating or dropping by parachute their agents—known as 'Fifth Columnists'— among the opposing defenders. How many, the authorities never knew, and it was tempting to not only assume they could be everywhere, but also, when things went wrong, it was easy to blame it on saboteurs.

After the war, the BBC aired a popular television series entitled *Foyle's War*, devoted to plots of treachery, covert enemy acts of terrorism and disruption of war industries.

My first experience of enemies on the Home Front had been in September while I was engaged in ground training at a former coastal summer resort. Every morning a Lysander—a useful RAF high-wing monoplane employed mostly as an artillery spotter by the Army—flew low up and down the coast. We got quite used to it until one morning two Hurricane fighters flew close beside it and ordered it to land. The pilot—a German of course—thought better of it and got his gunner to fire at the two British aircraft from the rear cockpit. It had been captured like others in France during the confusion of Blitzkrieg and the abandonment of military stores and equipment. The Hurricanes promptly peeled off and, to the surprise of onlookers on the cliffs, shot it down into the sea.

But back to the soccer game. It must have become perfectly clear to any unauthorized listeners on the fighter station that our pilots would be away from their aircraft on that particular afternoon, for just two or three hours, for a bit of fun. Many civilian employees worked in and around the base and frequented the pubs in the evening.

A quick radio message to enemy intelligence provided an opportunity that was too good to pass up. The whole area would be temporarily undefended. As a result the German pilots had a field day with a clear run in and out.

It was an unforgivable breach of security and a stupid, but well meaning, bit of planning.

Posters went up all over Britain as the war progressed: "Careless Talk Costs Lives" and "The Enemy May Be Watching". Railway stations, post offices, Government buildings and town squares sprouted similar advice. With a dash of wry humour, the public became seriously aware of keeping their mouths shut about sensitive material. In fact Britain became obsessed with 'loose lips'.

The Irish (Eire or the Southern Irish Republic) were a leaky source of information to the enemy. Because of the long historical antagonistic relationship with the English, many in our nearest 'neutral country' sympathized with the German cause. Enemy U-boats were suspected of refuelling, resupplying or hiding in Western Irish ports—probably not so frequently as we then imagined. It was also quite easy for paid informers or saboteurs to slip across from the south into Northern Ireland, an integral part of the UK, and then legitimately make their way by ferry to the British mainland. Such contacts became the subject of numerous British adventure films.

There was one other rather bizarre event in this connection. The circumstances perhaps need some further explanation. I still think about it often.

With over six hundred airfields in commission within the United Kingdom at the height of the Second World War, it was not too difficult to make it over or through some of the perimeter fences. As time went on, the RAF Regiment was formed, expanded and trained as the military arm of the Air Force principally for aerodrome defence. In the early days, almost anyone could walk onto most airfields at will.

The incident that has vividly stayed with me occurred early in 1941. Our Squadron was about to take off on an operation just before noon. We all had our very important and carefully memorized cockpit routine check every time we individually took to the air. I did what I always did slowly and deliberately, before taxiing out in correct order, heading to the downwind end of the runway.

For some reason, which I will never know, I glanced down at my feet that rested on the rudder pedals. Because of the angle of the bright sunlight, I got a slight reflection from some metallic part that seemed somehow not quite usual. I nearly shrugged the feeling off, and then what I can only describe as a sixth sense took over.

I did what I had never done before. I wheeled my aircraft out of the pack, off to the side, returned to my dispersal area and, to the surprise of my ground crew, signalled to them to chock the wheels. I undid my straps, hopped out of the cockpit and laid my parachute on the edge of the wing.

Calling for a flashlight, I leaned into the dark shadows at the far end of the cockpit, and there to my amazement lay a large Z–shaped crank starter handle, wedged through and in between my two rudder pedals. There was absolutely no way it could have been left like that in the cockpit. It had no function there whatsoever, and even if it was dropped by sheer accident, it could not have been wedged the way it was.

Had I taken off that morning, just a few minutes before, I would have been travelling at full throttle down the runway and, at the right moment, I would have eased back my control column, as I always did, and expected to soar skywards.

Except on this occasion the large metal handle would have successfully blocked my elevator cable from moving backwards. I would then have gone straight ahead, right through the metal doors of the large hangar situated just a few hundred feet from the end of the runway in use.

I was understandably puzzled and, to be truthful, somewhat shaken. I needed to have someone else to take a look. I called the flight sergeant i.c. maintenance, who wisely put a guard on the aircraft. The Squadron that had left me behind of course returned eventually after the mission with questions about where I had gone. The CO was summoned and he regarded the matter with the utmost seriousness.

The military police were called. The same afternoon an arrest was made. As so often is the case in such strange incidents, no publicity was given to the event. There was no official report or explanation forthcoming. The matter was dropped, and I heard no more about what was nearly – once again my very last flight.

15.

One Of My Big Mistakes (And Someone Else's Too)

November 18, 1941

We were young and very, very keen. We'd patrolled and completed a wide variety of tasks in the far north of Britain. We'd trained intensively—and a bit impatiently—from May to November, 1941. We'd waited to be posted to the hottest theatre of the air war, southeast of London, and now the call came from Fighter Command itself. We were finally going south!

I suppose we were a bit like a circus troupe all set to perform under the big top for the first time—before a seriously critical audience.

Our squadron, we told ourselves, was not only ready but good. We had lots of pride in our planes, in our ability to act and respond as a unit, and in ourselves. We had a superb commanding officer, a born leader whom we all respected. We'd make a cracking good show. We'd show 'em.

We took off very early from the suddenly deserted looking airfield near the northern tip of Scotland. The ground crews and administrative staff had all left by special train the previous day. A six hundred plus mile flight lay ahead of us, with one refuelling stop.

Our aircraft were all in tiptop shape, and our immaculate formation was a sight to behold, two flights of six aircraft in perfect formations. The plan included a gently, curving approach southwards to legendary Biggin Hill. We would peel off and land at ten second intervals and sweep up to our dispersal area where a smiling, applauding group of our very own ground crews would happily welcome us. *The new "124" had arrived. Big moment...*

Unfortunately nothing remotely like that happened. One and then another agonized voice screamed over the RT, "Balloons, balloons! Cables, balloons!"

The capital was protected in several ways. One of these was the famous, much photographed, Balloon Barrage—hundreds of blimps raised on steel cables from winches mounted on sturdy trucks.

The aim was to keep low-flying enemy planes from swooping in to target particular buildings or vital installations. Strict instructions had been issued that the barrage would be down as we closed into our destination, but someone had goofed for they were still in place. Those cables could slice through the wing of practically any plane. One more word was shouted into the ears of all the pilots, and that word was *scatter!*

We had to land individually. In the frantic melee that followed, miraculously, not a single Spitfire was damaged. We dropped out of the sky like a motley gaggle of trainees. On arrival we made a dismal sight. The impact was one of puzzled disgrace. Dejectedly we drifted into the mess in embarrassed and angry small groups. Yes, we were angry; it was *not* our fault!

After this inauspicious start, we were each escorted to our rooms. The Mess seemed to us more like a country hotel, with its imposing portico and where everyone was on their toes, smartly dressed and moving purposefully. Despite its frequent bombing attacks, morale was at a proud level. Everyone somehow was keen to offer help, to be co-operative. Someone remarked it appeared as if we had all died and gone to heaven.

One of the batmen—we suddenly felt quite important—who had grabbed my bag, preceded me into my room. I noticed the neatly made bed and a side table with a framed picture of a thoroughly wholesome looking girl, a chest of drawers, the top two units of which displayed a jumble of brushes, razors and tablets.

"I am so sorry sir," the flustered young man blurted out, "I have been so busy today. These are Flying Officer Martin's things. I should have cleared them out this morning."

"Who?" I started to ask.

"Sorry, Mr. Martin was killed this morning."

Early next day, we were ordered to be ready for action by seven am. We were now in Valhalla and we were expected to acquit ourselves well. Biggin Hill had the distinction of shooting down the most enemy aircraft to date—over 1,000 confirmed.

Our briefing indicated that we were to be introduced, slowly at first, to the storm and chaos of aerial operations on a grand scale. Some days we learned, along the Channel coast of south east England and northwest Europe, the number of aircraft in the air, allied and enemy, would be numbered not just in the scores, or the hundreds, but up to over two thousand. Today, therefore, we were to be part of a sizable formation, ordered to patrol and protect a large area of shipping. The German bases were only a mere forty miles away. We took off, feeling as though we were very small cogs in a very large machine. Now for my big mistake.

I should explain we had a radio on the left side of the cockpit, with a series of four buttons connecting the pilots to one of four channels, each of which, when pressed, had a different function and range. Just before the buttons was a small lever; push it forward your transmission was ON; pull it back, you ceased to transmit. One of our channels enabled each aircraft to communicate with the others in his own particular formation. The problem was that any pilot that left his transmitter ON prevented all of the rest of his formation from communicating completely in any direction.

We carried out our patrol, but my communication with the leader went dead. I got no special instructions, and I found that I could not raise anyone on the radio. *Oops!* I thought, *our first big show and we have an equipment malfunction.*

Eventually, after a few confusing hand signals, we landed. In the crew room there was a querulous buzz of conversation. Did someone leave the RT switch on? With foreboding I quickly nipped back to my Spitfire, peered into my cockpit and, with exquisite shame, realized it was me. Of course, I had to go back and own up—and deservedly got a very vociferous dressing-down with a colourful selection of appropriately unprintable words!

That was my first Biggin Hill operation. I felt I had to redeem myself. To be quite sure, I fitted a very strong elastic band wrapped around the transmission lever, with the other end anchored to the OFF side of the switch. Whenever I wanted to communicate, I always had to hold the lever to ON, and as soon as I had finished, it snapped itself back to the OFF position on its own.

One or two of the pilots quietly copied my brilliant idea, but I still had to live down my major error which could have endangered the operation had we been attacked, say from above.

So this has been about two big mistakes. One was certainly not my responsibility, but the other decidedly was.

I never made that mistake again.

16.

Two Requests For Volunteers

November 1941

One of the earliest rules given to raw recruits by knowledgeable old sweats—if they are willing to listen—is *never volunteer*.

It's early on for the eager young trainees. They have already discovered there are plenty of fatigues or penalties handed out—mostly unjust and always unpleasant. The Sergeant addresses the squad pleasantly, for a change. "Do any of you men know anything about motorcycles?"

Now probably very few could truthfully say, *yes, b*ut the lure of a less arduous activity is just too much of a temptation. Up shoot four hands. "I do Sarge," say the recruits attached to each of those hands.

"Good," says the benign NCO, "you four go and shovel out the latrines." There's a snigger of laughter. How could they be so dumb? But they won't fall for that line again.

However, in every branch of the active military, there will always be some call for volunteers—genuine ones—and usually there will be a response of some sort.

I can remember two calls for volunteers that were sent to appropriate RAF squadrons by the Air Ministry, and I signed up for both of them. There were of course 'carrots' attached to both offers, but I have often since wondered why I signed my name. Indeed why does anyone volunteer for desperate, hazardous or impossible missions? The history of both world wars is littered with such appeals. The press like to label the response as bravery—love of King and Country. That is too easy an answer. Ask any veteran who was faced with compelling requests or choices, whether they involved mini-submarines, air missions deep in enemy territory or small bands of face-blackened commandos assaulting a hostile coastline by landing craft.

Through talking to others and my own observations I would suggest there could be half a dozen motives, some praiseworthy perhaps and a few of the other kind. Let's look at the latter first.

Understand that most of those in action or on operational duty were *young*, they were fit—or been made that way—and they had been trained. When presented with an offer which appeared less mundane, more stimulating, more challenging, more adventurous; the lure of adventure tops the list when it comes to reasons why perfectly healthy young men (or women) put themselves deliberately in harm's way.

The war, with all its suffering and insecurity, its death and destruction, brings into the often monotonous lives of a nation's youngest and fittest adults an element of activity and danger. There is often created, then, an atmosphere of common purpose with an equally important new emotion which is probably the most lasting memory to which veterans bear witness—Comradeship—a new and powerful force for many.

Another motive—and I would have to admit to my share of this—is Foolhardiness. In the rush of response there was often an air of quick enthusiasm, devil-may-care, machismo, even bravado; or by contrast a negative feeling of hopelessness or resignation. Not much solid thought probably goes into such decisions to step forward and sign up. *What the hell*, says the able, adrenalized young person, *why not? Put me down.* Perhaps there is some merit in these choices, but probably not too much. There should be some room here for the ingredient of family responsibility also; *I don't have to step forward, do I?*

There is another quite frequent cause for apparent daring. Put simply, it would be difficult to classify it as at all praiseworthy; that's Ignorance.

I have watched people offer themselves without the slightest attempt to find out pertinent details concerning the mission or their own suitability. They just couldn't be bothered to ask or enquire. The acceptance was irresponsible and as such one would wonder what sort of quality the volunteer possessed.

By contrast there is nothing but admiration, in the first instance, for an individual who listens, appraises, diligently considers and then puts his safety, even his life perhaps on the line. I said 'in the first instance' advisedly because there was quite often an aura of inevitability in an appeal for volunteers. It was not at times unusual for bravery to be confused with depression. For a variety of causes—a family death, a devastating letter, etc.—the volunteer is suicidal and this route is an easy solution. Counselling, where it is possible, is in order if this situation is recognized. Especially so is an irrational decision a good basis for effective, even if apparently noble, action.

The last type of gallantry could be the *special mission syndrome*. The individual is not so much a volunteer as a willing participant. He or she may be the only one available with the necessary expertise, knowledge or skills. To say yes when approached with full knowledge of the hazards and the personal and family sacrifice involved can be often of the very highest order of valour and altruism.

Only the individual knows for sure just where he or she stands. In what category is it correct to be labelled? I recall a fellow student in my high school who appeared to be, in any sport he participated, utterly fearless. I remember we used to say, *if ever there is a war, he will probably grab a machine gun and single-handedly charge an enemy bastion, destroy the opposition thoroughly and achieve the objective*—and that is exactly what he did!

Then there were other individuals who were utterly paralysed with fear; yet went ahead and did the job in spite of everything.

So, for myself, there were these two situations: From my present vantage point I can clearly describe them, but I can't dispassionately assess where the quality or otherwise of my participation could have been gauged. Mercifully I was rejected for both.

The first was an offer I had never heard of before, and it had a real hook. The deal went like this: in our theatre of war, there were too many precious cargo vessels from North America—packed with vital war materials—being attacked and sunk by U-boats or enemy bombers. The top brass came up with the idea of putting powerful catapults on the bows of larger merchant ships travelling in convoys, particularly those heading for the Northwest Soviet port of Murmansk, a passage with deadly Arctic weather.

When warning of attack was received, a fighter—Spitfire or Hurricane—would be launched into the air and engage the enemy. At the end of the encounter, the pilot would climb several thousand feet to well ahead of the convoy and then bale out. After a 'wet landing' one of the ships would pick up the pilot from the water as they sailed by. Hopefully attacks would be warded off and ships saved, all for the cost of one fighter lost—a good bargain. Simple.

Unfortunately there was a flaw in the scenario—in fact several flaws. Convoys don't steam in a straight line—they zigzag frequently to avoid U-boats and radar. Also the temperature of the ocean in those northern latitudes was such that maximum survival time was about four minutes; a human body would almost certainly be dead long before the nearest ship might reach him. Lastly, due to the constant danger of underwater attack, all ships were expressly prohibited from 'heaving to' even briefly, to pick up anyone, even their own comrades who might be struggling in the water after being torpedoed.

And the hook, the inducement? We were told that the Navy and especially the Merchant Navy fed well. The rumour was there was no food rationing on board; crews were too important so they lived in the galley like kings—or so went the story!

The idea was also tried elsewhere, but with practically no success. At best it was a pure suicide mission.

It was general practice to move squadrons of aircraft, often at short notice, to where they were most needed. Ours had been ordered down from Scotland late in 1941 to the legendary Battle of Britain station, Biggin Hill, just south of London, which had claimed at that time nearly 1,000 enemy plane *kills*. As a result, my volunteer junket was cancelled.

The second appeal, or I should say posting, was not much safer. This was in the Mediterranean where the sea was decidedly warmer. The destination for the convoys was Malta, a vital strategic sea and air base just south of Sicily. It had the unenviable reputation of being the most bombed piece of real estate on the whole allied side. It suffered an average three bombing raids per day for nearly three years. It was too far to reinforce the defensive fighter squadrons stationed there by flying direct from England and across Nazi occupied France. The planes had to be taken by sea. Several of the planes and pilots were split off from my own squadron, and I was one to be scheduled for this somewhat dicey operation. This was risky not just because of the distance but also it was extremely difficult to take off or land a Spitfire on a heaving deck when you could not see straight ahead due to the shape of the tilted nose.

The method selected was to load forty-seven precious Spitfires onto the old American aircraft carrier, *Wasp*. Starting from England, it headed for North Africa, then from near Algiers, late at night, the carrier steamed full speed towards Malta, and at dawn the planes took off and made a 600 mile dash to the beleaguered base before their presence was discovered. This occurred on the 20th of April, 1942 and was by far the largest shipment of reinforcements to date at that time.

The planes made it but unfortunately not for long. Many were destroyed on the ground within a few days before they could be put into use. Nearly all of the pilots involved reached Malta but most one by one were shot down, killed or missing within a few weeks. Fortunately for me, before the planned departure from UK, my own participation was pre-empted by being wounded, returning from another operation on the coast of France.

Once again I dodged the bullet—well, for a short time.

Pity in a way—we had been told that the beaches were great and the swimming was wonderful. The air raid shelters were also amongst the safest in the world because the limestone island was honeycombed with caves—of course this would have been of no use to me if I was up in the air when bombs were falling.

These were two destinations in my flying career for which I was heartily glad to be turned down.

17.

Sometimes We Can Celebrate Our Failures

November 1941; 2008

I can relive my emotions, and I can recall every detail as I sat in my cramped cockpit on that freezing November day in Southern England.

As seniors we do have quite a lot more time now to remember. Maybe our brain cells are of a higher quality the further back we go? It is amazing how past images come up on our mental screens. I am pulling up one right now: *it was the day I was wounded in World War II.*

Our Spitfire squadron had been briefed to take off at dawn to cover the withdrawal of a small British commando raid—mostly for intelligence gathering—from the Nazi occupied coast of France. We waited and waited. Meanwhile the poor Army guys had been tossing about on a very choppy sea for even longer because a rendezvous for the landing craft had been missed; seldom did such things go according to plan. When the word to go at last came to our Squadron Commander, the weather had turned really foul, visibility was at a minimum, and soon our formation got lost. Backwards and forwards we went finding it mighty difficult to keep station in the murky conditions; especially to spot small, camouflaged LCI's bobbing about below us. Fuel became dangerously low and an emergency landing was indicated at a forward base airfield on the English coast.

That kind of rapid descent had been particularly practiced by the Squadron. On this day, however we had inherited a very capable pilot from Czechoslovakia—any who were able to escape from Europe to Britain were welcome—and this was his first operation with us.

Unfortunately he spoke very little English. In the low clouds, his aircraft and mine collided. Down I went.

In such a situation everything happens in split seconds. It is all so totally unexpected. One moment I was trying to follow the plane just ahead of me heading towards the small airfield, the next my controls had totally vanished. No time to bail out. Right up to the actual point of impact, I can still replay that dive in my mind; the ground coming up to meet me, just like a compressed film. It might just have occurred yesterday.

What followed was an intermittent series of confused images and time sequences, ambulances, hospitals, nurses, surgeons. Watchers on the ground, all from quite different perspectives, each gave their own account.

My actual survival was unexpected. The rate was—and still is—quite small for any mid-air collision. The Air Force didn't even rush to send a blood wagon. At that time the event was not in the least remarkable. Aircraft were falling out of the sky, for one reason or another, every day in 1941.

Our Squadron had only recently moved south into the thick of the fighting. We were just boys really, mostly eighteen, nineteen or twenty. We had trained hard for some months while we were engaged in naval protection to the North and thought that we were at the peak of our performance. We were quietly proud of ourselves; I don't recall that we felt particularly brave, as the press insisted; scared stiff would often be much closer to the truth. We just happened to be born for that time.

Little did we know that these small operations on the English coast might be playing an infinitesimal part in preparation for the D-Day invasion three long years later on the Normandy coast.

As I lay in an Air Force ward for several months my uppermost thought was that I had failed.

At that time our tactics required that we fly in formations made up of sets of pairs. My No. 2 and very good friend, Mike, soon went on to be appointed Squadron Leader, to gain gongs—medals—and to do what we had been trained for, which is to say shoot down German aircraft. I on the other hand was lying horizontal in a bed with bits of metal stuck in and around me. *Why hadn't I seen that other aircraft coming up behind me?*

I'd have been silently gnashing my teeth, except that I didn't have any; the microphone at the end of my oxygen mask had gone through my mouth and neatly caused the removal of every item of my oral furniture in quick time. Much later I recognized that this was one of the greatest benefits of my personal war. My last ever dental appointment was 78 years ago—that adds up over the years to quite a savings.

Two generations later I visited the exact spot where the Spitfire buried its nose in a hedgerow. That too was indelibly etched in my brain. My son, who had flown over from Canada with me, dug around, and sure enough there was a piece of green aluminum embedded like a fossil that could only have come from a Spitfire!

It took me years to throw off that sense of failure.

There were about twenty of us and we were a team. I went on to fly again, but only to help train others. For me the days of my tension-packed career were gone. Just after the Battle of Britain, the 1940 period, there was quite a bit of glamour towards fighter pilots in the United Kingdom. Naturally in times of high casualties there were more and more rank openings to move into, but I never got promoted in Fighter Command to Squadron Leader as my No. 2 did.

Our squadron eventually lost fifty-two pilots. Fifty-two young men killed, one of them, sadly, was the one who had collided with me. He was shot down over Northern France a short while later by a Focke-Wulf 190.

Years later in the classroom, and still later as an ancient veteran at Remembrance time in November, I would find myself answering the usual question from eager young students: "How many did you shoot down, sir?"

"None," I would say; I almost felt like hanging my head in shame. For a time I struggled with rather lame answers; *lots of players never score a touchdown... I like to think I helped to protect some other people... I saved other lives and carried out some routine assignments...* etc.

It was a long time before I came to realize there was a good answer of which I could legitimately feel some pride. I learned to say, forthrightly, that I was glad I had not been directly and wittingly the cause of death of someone's son, brother, father or husband. My eight wing machine guns could pour out a hail of .303 bullets at the rate of 160 per second that could make a real mess of any target.

Had I known them personally, what a horror that would be to have on my conscience, watching their Messerschmitt go down in flames. The world, in some ways, may have changed for the better. I hope so, but the entertainment industry still too often glorifies warfare. I often think that my own feelings are an illustration of how wrongly we can interpret events or rearrange priorities. It does teach me to examine myself more carefully and, in all aspects of my life, to consider my motives truthfully—war or no war.

Anyway my lack of success as a 'movie fighter ace' led me to University and a teaching career. Not only did I survive the war—survival was, as several of my vet friends declare, our major achievement—but I went on to lecture to numbers of trainees, and I found I enjoyed it.

Looking back at it, my year in hospital actually proved a good experience. After six and a half years, I left the Services for good and later on started on a new phase of my life: I headed for tropical Africa with my young family—but that too is another story.

Central RAF hospital, Halton, Bedfordshire (No longer in existence)

18.

Upstaging Winston Churchill

April 23, 1942

April 23rd, 1942 seemed like any other uneventful day in the Second World War. I was quietly enjoying my hard regulation bed in one of the orthopaedic wards of the largest RAF hospital in Britain.

Suddenly a warrant officer burst into the ward and breathlessly announced that six *suitably wounded* airmen were required to travel up to London that very evening to be present at a patriotic spectacular entitled *Battle For Freedom*, which was to be held at the ten thousand-seat Royal Albert Hall and organized by the *Daily Express,* probably the largest of the national newspapers.

Since we were all in pyjamas or hospital gowns, orderlies were sent scurrying to the storage below to retrieve our uniforms. We knew nothing whatsoever about this event, so we were happy, if somewhat bemused, to be selected as volunteers. Any change in the monotony of a dreary hospital routine, where all the windows were covered by sandbags to protect from flying glass, was obviously welcome.

A whirl of activity followed; a truck arrived to take us to the train station, then a quick trip to the City, then three taxis weaving through huge areas of rubble and bombed out buildings. On arrival at the famous Hall, we climbed with our crutches and sticks to the level where a box of exceedingly good seats had been reserved for us. We proceeded to take off our ties, shed tunics, loosen our collars and prepare to settle ourselves as well as we could.

The building was crammed full with representatives from every imaginable type of Service, men and women, military and civilian.

First came the introduction of dignitaries. The Royal Box, with bemedalled princes, was suitably applauded. About fifty feet away, just to the left of us, the Right Honourable Winston Churchill accompanied by his wife and daughter Sgt. Mary Churchill. Winnie stood, bathed in spotlights, as he removed his ever-present cigar and gave the 'V' sign to loud cheers. Next the film star announcer asked the audience to recognize eleven World War I Victoria Cross winners—the highest accolade for bravery in the British Commonwealth. The group stood with quiet dignity while the sold-out crowd applauded enthusiastically in an obvious atmosphere of awe and respect.

At this juncture our little group, average age about twenty-two, were wishing the show would get started and we could sink down back again into our somewhat uncomfortable perches.

"We have one more treat for you," announced the MC from the stage. "With us are a group of Battle of Britain flyers who have been taking on the Luftwaffe in the skies above us..."

"Come on," we muttered to ourselves, craning our necks to see where these aircrew would be seated. Suddenly every searchlight in the huge circular amphitheatre swung around this time to bathe in dazzling light our motley looking crew, a decidedly scruffy bunch entangled with their chairs and sticks. The whole audience stood and cheered us to the rafters. None of us had been advised that we were to be any-thing other than spectators. I can remember seeing Winnie applauding us from a mere bus length away. I think each of us would like to have made it clear that we were not part of that incredibly outnumbered group of Spitfire and Hurricane squadrons who did so much to save England from invasion nearly two years before.

The stirring programme finally got under way with displays of military precision, songs, nostalgic poetry, choirs, massed-bands and exhortations to march on to total victory. I confess that, after we had got over our acute embarrassment, we kept resorting to outbreaks of uncontrolled giggles.

Only we knew that practically everyone of the *suitably wounded airmen* had broken arms or legs in very undramatic accidents, some the result of falling down the stairs when intoxicated. In fact, I was the only one of the group who had been legitimately wounded following an operation over the English Channel some months before!

I still have the programme of the event (price sixpence) and copies of the next day's full page newspaper report with photos of the 'vast throng' of loyal subjects of which I was genuinely proud to be a part. This event provided a splash of colour and enthusiasm in what history has called some of Britain's darkest days of World War II.

THE ROYAL ALBERT HALL

MANAGER: REGINALD ASKEW

BATTLE

FOR

FREEDOM

'URGENCY IN DECISION,
SPEED IN THE ATTACK,
COURAGE IN FACE OF THE ENEMY'

PRESENTED BY THE 'DAILY EXPRESS'
ON SAINT GEORGE'S DAY, 1942

FOR SERVICE D CHARITIES

At the Royal Albert Hall

1942 Winston Churchill and daughter Mary

Lawrence Olivier in The Dedication : Picture, Back Page.

BRITAIN MARCHES

Daily Express Pageant of the Good Fight

By WILLIAM BARKLEY

IN the Albert Hall last evening we saw our-selves. For the first time in this war great and glorious companies of our men and women marched and counter-marched before our eyes with banners flying.

No longer was the war a State secret. We were permitted to know, and see and proclaim, our heroes and our heroines.

The pageant—Battle for Freedom—was described by the commentator, Major Christopher Stone, D.S.O., M.C., as the work of the back-room boys of the Daily Express.

Certainly they provided the bones. but the flesh and blood were the living men and women of all the British and Empire Services and of the Allied and United Nations.

Many of them had come from battle. All were going to battle.

LIGHT ON HEROES

The vast audience greeted them as men and women sym-bolising the good fight, dedicated to victory in a noble and splen-did simplicity, and arousing emotions in which every man and woman who saw the display re-dedicated themselves to the same task.

We seemed to become one great family, taking joy and pride in our achievements.

First the limelight spotted veri-table heroes. Nine men stood up in a box toegther—every one the winner of a Victoria Cross.

They stood there with dignity, but with the modest bearing we expect. as they were saluted with the applause of the multitude. Then two Canadian V.C.s were picked out.

GERMANS FREE 35 MORE

VICHY. Thursday.—The execu-tion of 15 more Jews and Com-munists was cancelled by the Germans in Paris today. Twenty hostages at St. Nazaire have been released.

De Brinon. Vichy representative in Paris, congratulated two French workmen tonight for handing over Frenchmen who attacked a German soldier.—B.U.P.

Cold

Straits : Cold ; overcast.

RUSSIA LO

'Second front

Express Staff Rep

VICE - COMMISSAR LOZOVSKY raised by d of a second front in Europ in the Soviet Foreign Office

He said : "The U.S.S.R. fight alone against the Ax

Newspaper cuttings

Royal Albert Hall, London 1942

19.

A Tranquil Seaside Resort

May to October 1942; 1943; 1993.

I went up to the desk manager and asked if he had any historical leaflet concerning the building in which he worked, particularly the period of the Second World War; maybe it was bombed in the '40s? He stared at me blankly then assured me that he didn't think that it had any such past. I suggested he ask some of his colleagues; reluctantly he wandered to two or three of the older clerks, but it was clear they knew nothing whatsoever of any significance; it was after all before practically any of them had been born.

I arrived at the Palace Hotel on my birthday in 1942. It was not for a holiday though it might have looked like it. Its WWII name was RAF Officers' Hospital, Torquay. It was my third hospital since I was wounded as a Spitfire Pilot the previous year.

Set on the rocky shores of nearly circular Torbay in Southwest England, this well-known holiday resort and spa encompassed four small towns and a number of villages—Brixham, the most historical; Paignton, with most of the major hotels taken over for military use and where rehearsals for D-Day were held on local beaches; fashionable Torquay itself; and high on the cliff to the north, Babbacombe, where many aircrew trainees—myself included—were kitted out at the reception centre and started their service in the early days of the war.

The whole area would have been thought of as quiet, mild and secluded with the occasional unexpected palm tree along the promenade—almost sleepy. Yet like many stretches of the south coast of England it was subjected to air attacks by the Luftwaffe operating from

Nazi-occupied France. One hundred and sixty-eight civilians were recorded as killed and many more seriously wounded, including a number of children who had been evacuated from the London blitz.

When our rigorous daily dose of therapy was over, the 'walking wounded' were permitted to catch transport from just outside the main entrance. My girlfriend, Kay, had secured a week's leave from her Government job, and like many other relatives of patients, she was able to stay in a nearby B&B.

It was on a sunny afternoon in June when we boarded a bus marked Harbour Front. Despite a grim war being in process—and not too far away—the seafront was quite crowded, a mixture of shoppers, elderly ladies from the town's many retirement homes, and couples from some of the few hotels that were still operating.

I was travelling on crutches, in uniform of course, and there was plenty of time, so we were not hurrying. Passing a small jeweller's shop, we paused and glanced in the window at a large velvet-covered tray with a selection of rings. We looked at each other, then glanced again. I hobbled in beside her, examined a few for style—and price—and in a few minutes we were walking out again with the engagement band on her appropriate finger and a somewhat self-conscious smile on our faces. We secured a 'cuppa' in a small teashop, lingering not so much over the seldom available iced 'fancy cakes' as over the sight of the ring where it should be. I felt like a very mature twenty year old! We arrived at the bus stop for the return, and I was about to gingerly hoist myself aboard when I heard the sound of aircraft.

Because of my type of service, it instantly registered that those were not British so I stayed where I was with one hand still on the step banister. The sound grew louder and suddenly with a deafening roar three ME 109's in V formation swept over the top of us at rooftop height. The black crosses were clearly visible on the underside of the wings.

I saw no point in shouting a warning because the three German fighters were heading straight out to sea, but I kept my eye on them as they sped over the water flying at about a hundred feet or less. Such incursions by enemy planes along the south and eastern coasts of England were daily occurrences. I could do nothing about these very unfriendly visitors—this time I wasn't in the cockpit. I was just like a civilian onlooker. I was about to pull myself upright into the bus when the three fighter planes—almost out of sight—suddenly wheeled in a 180 degree tight turn and headed straight back towards the crowded part of the waterfront, and exactly where we were standing.

I only just managed to let out the loudest yell I could muster—something like 'Everyone take cover immediately...we are about to be attacked by enemy planes'—before the first bullets arrived. Some folk on the waiting bus crouched down below the level of the windows, which of course provided no protection whatever.

Across the road, by the seawall, were three long hastily-constructed surface air raid shelters. The concrete blocks could provide some safety. My wife-to-be with commendable presence of mind started to shoo or shove many of the mostly elderly nearby towards the entrances. Just behind the bus was a department store with three large display windows. All three planes now in line abreast were raking the road with all their guns spitting flame. The first sounds of what suddenly became total pandemonium were the shattering of each of those tall windows. Then came the chattering of the synchronized machine guns, the screams of the civilians were followed by the dropping of six anti-personnel bombs, two from each aircraft; nearly all of this chaos occurred almost simultaneously. Finally came the roaring crescendo of the three engines as they once again passed directly over us at full throttle.

The whole raid was over in less than thirty seconds. In its wake could be heard the moaning from those who had unfortunately been hit, crying of children and confused shouting for help for the scattered casualties. The shelters filled up quickly in case the planes returned, but the attackers had decided to head for their base before the official alarm was raised and our defences, such as they were then, went into counteraction.

Ambulances, two fire engines with dignified clanging, and auxiliary police started to congregate at the waterfront. Within five minutes, the dead were discretely moved aside and covered—usually with their own coats. Tow trucks hitched up damaged cars and the smashed-up bus was towed away. Clerks came out of stores and started to sweep up piles of broken glass. Another bus eventually arrived and we resumed our ride back to the hospital. Looking back—and I did not realize it at the time—little seemed to have changed. Traffic flowed quietly while dogs barked, children played, and housewives continued to fill the baskets on their arms. It was as if, except in that immediate area, nothing had really happened. It probably did not rate a specific reference on the BBC evening news. This was not the front line, but still, in its own unobtrusive way, Torquay was at war.

Meanwhile the RAF hospital continued to operate as usual. It was full to capacity with several hundred aircrew; many soon after their rehabilitation would return to full operational duties. There was a large red cross on the roof and most of us felt, as we looked around our surroundings, pretty fortunate. The food was far better than on most regular units—they had actually kept on a few of the peacetime chefs.

Some of the rigorous therapy sessions, when we sweated to get our stiffened limbs flexing again, were held on the beach just below the old hotel gardens.

It became obvious, as time went on, that the Germans had quite an efficient intelligence network to keep them aware of juicy targets that were quite separate from the obvious industrial areas and transportation hubs. It was not unusual for the British to blame the southern Irish (Eire) for this state of affairs as it was not difficult for them to travel backwards and forwards to the UK. A number of towns of historical importance, residential quality for retirement or holiday significance were selected by the enemy, not for military reasons, but almost exclusively to terrorize the civilian population and especially because they were virtually undefended. Hitler reportedly personally picked out the targets in retaliation for one such old German town—Lübeck—attacked by the RAF. Such attacks were christened Baedeker raids, after the well-known tourist guides: Canterbury, Norwich, Exeter, Bath were examples and Torquay could be put in this category. From a cynically practical point of view, such a target as the Palace Hotel was a legitimate selection—even if it was totally against the Geneva Convention.

On the 25th of October, the hospital was bombed for the first time. About sixty-four were killed or seriously wounded; fortunately it occurred on a Sunday, the only day when the basement clinics were not in operation, otherwise there would have been a heavy loss of life. The cheery young auxiliary nurse who brought my breakfast to the room every day for four months was one of those killed. I had, by this time, just been sent to another hospital further north, but I have pictures of a large empty space where my room had been located—rather like a giant knife making two parallel cuts down a five layer cake.

On a second raid, soon after, the damage was much more extensive and the building was abandoned. All the remaining medical staff who survived had been dispersed and posted to other hospitals.

So as I walked through the once-again plush lobby and stately rooms, it was all too easy to be back where all was bustle and the mending of broken bodies, where the clients all wore blue and the nurses were dressed in crisp uniforms with their ranking headgear. Wandering outside, within the town, you could almost hear the tramp of thousands of feet pounding the pavement outside the lines of small hotels, around the bay, where the future aircrew were put through their rapid boot camp as the Americans call it—so many of whom were soon to perish in the skies of Europe, the deserts of North Africa and over the jungles of Burma.

Tranquil once again, I thought, *but a far cry from the unimaginable, mostly unremembered bursts, of activity of its wartime past.*

The Palace Hotel, Torquay (pre-war). During
WW11 The RAF Officers' Hospital

The Officers' hospital, 1942

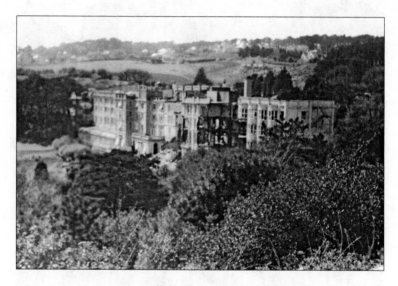

The RAF hospital after the first air raid (my
room was somewhere in the gap?)

Where my room was?

Shortly after my hospital stay, with my sister who
served as a nurse and an ambulance driver

Wedding day – Richard and Kay

20.

I'm Still Waiting For The Bill From The U.S. Army Air Corps

November 1943

Come on, darn you, get airborne! What's the matter with you? Fly, for goodness sake. Fly...

It just wouldn't. I had just started to take off in my bright yellow plane; I had a student behind me. I pulled back once more on the control column, but there was virtually no response. The plane was giving a series of fluttering jerks, like a bird with only half a wing. I had checked the wind direction...varying, certainly not perfect but seemed good enough.

A sea of aircraft were parked straight in front of me, in neat rows with military precision, bombers, fighters, carrier-borne and many others—all brand new—several scores of them.

My throttle was fully forward, but the stick was loose in my right hand. I thought for a moment it was airborne, that maybe the old girl was going to make it and with a burst of power just jump over the first row. It felt as if my plane was flying through a pool of treacle.

The wheels bounced on the ground—or on something else below me—and then again another bounce. The nose went up and a P14 Lightning passed just under my port side. The engine seemed to give a throaty, despairing sound, as if it was dying, gasping for breath. The control column was still limp and did not respond to my coaxing at all. I had too little flying speed; I could see an open space a little way beyond, but now it was really sinking and my nose was pointing too high—too high for me to see anything ahead—a proper stall.

There was a slight tearing sound as I hit the vertical tail of a Seamew, another plane directly below me.

Then a sickening thud, and more camouflaged metal started to fly past my cockpit. Although events were happening in sequence they also seemed to be taking place simultaneously. I sunk down like an uncooked pancake. As in other mishaps that I had experienced, there was a sudden silence. My engine had obviously cut out, probably when the propeller hit the ground, and all around me were various shapes and sizes of unfamiliar metal, grass, mud and debris—certainly where none of it should have been at all.

The silence did not last very long. I could soon hear voices, the sound of vehicles heading in my direction—and in my head I kept hearing an inner voice saying, "*What have you done? How could you possibly have landed in such an unfortunate spot?*" Then I started to think of that word, *responsibility*, and my stomach turned to water.

A small inner voice spoke up in my defence. "*It's not your fault. It's the stupid engine. There's something wrong with the motor because it didn't, wouldn't, respond. Yes, I'll be able to clear my name.*" These thoughts in quick succession probably took no more than a few seconds to scurry through my brain.

My first rational thought should have been to turn around and see if my trainee in the rear cockpit was unhurt. Fortunately he was alive and well—neither he nor I suffered more than a few cuts and bruises—though he was probably somewhat mystified at the turn of events. He had expected a smooth start to the flight, a steady, climbing corkscrew to our operational altitude and then a navigational exercise he was scheduled to work on.

There followed in sequence some predictable events whenever there is an accident: arrival of the fire wagon, the ambulance, ground crew running up with questions and so on.

The day had started quite normally like many for the last few months. Not long before I had finished about a year in hospital, after being wounded in a Spitfire mission off the coast of France. This therefore was really quite a soft job that I had landed, and even though I still greatly missed the action and the comradeship of the squadron that I had had to leave, I was quite enjoying myself in the new training role. Here I was flying in the morning with trainee cadets, giving lectures to classes in the afternoon and living quite close to the unit with my new wife. My current location was in sharp contrast to the whole coastline, now crammed with men and materials just poised to land somewhere in Northern Europe when the word was given—the details were still a closely guarded secret at that time.

In due course, from the dispersal area, where she had witnessed the occurrence, my civilian Air Ministry driver, 'Stewie' as everyone called her, promptly appeared with my Humber Snipe. This vehicle was large enough to take several trainees from our unit in the City the six miles or so to the Liverpool airport where I kept our training plane.

This driver, wearing her regulation dark blue overcoat and peaked hat was at my disposal with the car whenever I needed transportation. Not many guys my age or rank had the luxury of a staff car on call. Miss Stewart was a willing girl who was always punctual and co-operative. She must have read a lot of novels while waiting for my flights to finish. She had a ready smile and most of the time wore a cheerful but quizzical expression. I don't recall any comments that she made that morning, but on reflection she must have been somewhat taken aback when her own Officer Pilot climbed into his cockpit, took off with his student navigator and promptly seemed to flop down like a black swan in the midst of a gaggle of brand new, freshly painted warplanes belonging to the United States Air Force.

The port of Liverpool, with its miles of docks, was probably the largest and busiest cargo port at that time in all of Britain. Convoys regularly tied up from their hazardous U-boat fraught trip across the Atlantic from Halifax. Shipping was scarce and as soon as they had disgorged their vital supplies of war material, tanks, guns, vehicles, tools and of course food, they were turned round fast restocked and if necessary repaired for another transatlantic passage. Not all the West-to-East cargo however was in the hold. On deck were huge crates lined up and lashed together like a lot of toy bricks. Each container held one aircraft, packed tightly with the wings folded snugly along the fuselage and any of the empty spaces full of spare parts. Ironically, I was seeing these crates from a different angle now. Earlier in the war, as a Spitfire pilot on a Northern Scottish base, I had had a spell of escorting some of these convoys as they approached the UK. I even saw some of the wreckage that the German torpedoes caused in the fiercely fought Battle of the Atlantic, including a few of those very same smashed-up crates.

When the crates were opened and the planes carefully extracted on rollers and reassembled, those empties were often delivered to airfields, ports and factories as excellent, waterproof storage facilities. I actually lived and worked from one myself for a time. It was some of those aircraft that had just been delivered from Liverpool docks and were standing in neat rows that I had *chosen* to land on top of.

Naturally I had to report my event to the station headquarters. I wrote a brief report and arranged for my airplane to be collected and towed away for repair, if possible.

When I got back to my unit, however, I had to do much more explaining, and according to RAF protocol, I knew I would be the subject of a court of inquiry.

Considering that at this stage of the war there were nearly five hundred airfields in operation and several thousand planes in action, with hundreds being lost, crashed and missing every week, my little event was hardly worth a mention.

But procedure had to be followed. My log book was duly endorsed as it appeared to be a case clearly of gross carelessness—in other words a black eye. I expected no less. However for some time I couldn't stop questioning myself as to what really did happen. There is a dreamlike quality of mind that surrounds any unfortunate aerial accident. It all happened so quickly, and yet part of it seems to be in slow motion. *What could I have done differently? Was there another factor involved that might not be recognized, something that could not be proved, or disproved? Was there water in the petrol that caused the engine to stutter and falter? Did someone leave the fuel cap too loosely secured? Did the plugs need replacing? Should I not have taxied around the outside of all those parked planes, rather than taking off, even with a slight crosswind, beside them, when there appeared to be plenty of room and where I had often done so before?*

I had to tell the truth in my report, but what was the truth?

Up to that time I'd had a successful career and apparently acquitted myself reasonably well; I received consistently above-average assessments, and later a special citation. Even though I'd had three crashes, I'd not been judged blameworthy in any of them. Even still, I had to admit that I probably could have avoided the accident if I had been more super-careful with that wind. It's hard to say. Though it could be regarded as a stain on my reputation, I nevertheless continued to fly for another one and a half years.

Lecturing at age twenty-one was quite a new activity for me. Although I didn't know it at the time, this turned out to be a valuable episode in my life. I found myself teaching regularly a syllabus—the first significant step in what was to be a forty year career in education. I increasingly found myself enjoying the challenge.

Fortunately I didn't have to pay the tab to replace an RAF plane or send a cheque for the damage to the Government of the United States for a couple of their war planes!

Considering the speed at which war supplies were arriving in the choked bases of the British Isles, I very much doubt that anyone would even have missed a couple.

A Spitfire 1X B with the black and white Normandy Invasion
security markings (by this time I was instructing others)

21.

Escape! Help For Downed World War II Flyers

1971

"Go on, Dad, open it," pleaded my daughter. "It will be fun to see what they'd put in it all those years ago".

It was a smallish plastic container, five inches by six and approximately two inches tall. It was opaque and sealed with a now dirty strip of adhesive linen. We were all up at the cottage, and it was a wet afternoon. While rummaging in an old camping bag, this curious object had tumbled out onto the floor.

My memory was hazy, but I thought it was a first aid package. Being slightly concave, it was possibly designed to fit into a pocket of flying overalls. I remember it had been issued to aircrew for carrying with them on operations during the Second World War.

We pushed back the supper dishes, turned up the lamp and gently pried open the lid. It seemed at first to be full of fine, rust-coloured powder. Carefully poking about with a fork, we found a collection of odd shapes and yellowing paper below. Slowly recognition returned. It was not a first aid kit, although as pilots we often carried those as well. It was an Escape Kit—the RAF's answer to the knotty problem of *what do I do now?*

Imagine being caught in the unfortunate position of climbing out of a downed aircraft in enemy controlled territory or floating apprehensively earthwards at the end of a parachute over the not-so-welcoming fields of Northern Europe in the 1940's. I could still hear the laughter that greeted some of the items of the backroom boys' latest brain-child when it was first hatched. I remember the day when the contents had been solemnly lifted out one by one from the demonstrator prototype by a somewhat embarrassed intelligence officer. Members of the Squadron sat on benches in the briefing room with a mixture of amusement and disbelief.

Some of the items certainly had their value—and were later to prove it. Others struck us as a trifle bizarre, if not downright hilarious. Escape Kits of course had changed over the years to suit different theatres of war, military policies, local initiatives and personal preference. All had been part of attempts to save lives—and precious training dollars—enabling survival, escape and return to duty.

Flying over enemy territory, huge numbers of aircrews were lost, but scores did successfully make it back—utilizing their own ingenuity and paraphernalia—from below the crowded skies of Europe, the vastness of North African deserts and later the mountains of Korea and the hell of Vietnam. Although all personnel were supposed to try to escape, thousands more felt it was dangerously impractical. In disguise, there were greater odds of being shot as a spy.

Some flew just with the bare essentials provided to all aircrew: inflatable rubber dinghies, yellow 'Mae West' life jackets, sea marker dyes, shark repellents, and the like. Some others added their own 'reversible' uniforms, even pyjamas, in order to look as if they were in civilian clothes. Some had counterfeit local money sewn into their uniform linings, and a variety of harmless looking survival devices that were, in emergencies, surprisingly useful or lethal.

Some pilots went aloft draped like a Christmas tree! A few superstitiously added a good luck charm.

Escapees sometimes preferred to go it alone and returned independently after several weeks on the run; others were able to contact members of the Resistance through a password which was regularly changed and made available at briefings. For patriots to make themselves vulnerable to arrest, torture and often death was in itself an act of great personal courage and heroism in occupied countries of Europe. If aircrew followed correct procedure this would get themselves hopefully onto one of the underground *ladders*, such as from Northern France via the passes over the Pyrenees Mountains and finally a pickup by a British submarine off the coast of Spain. Many made it by such a route.

Preplanning gave a man a measure of confidence. This now rotting little plastic box on the table was an echo from the past and then, as now, was greeted with rapt interest. "So this," I explained to my family, "was just one addition to our catalogue of personal equipment—a checklist of items, essential and optional, that we carried on missions. As the War progressed the list grew even longer."

Defending combat squadrons usually had their pilots in three modes: *Release* meant you were off duty but could easily be contacted if necessary; *Available Standby* meant you had to be able to take off at ten, fifteen, or twenty minutes' notice; *Readiness* meant that when the 'scramble' call came everything and everybody leaped into action. Pilots and crew would be relaxing in chairs in full flying gear, but within a maximum of three minutes had to be at 'Angels Ten' (10,000 feet) and talking to base on the right channel. This took a great deal of practice to achieve.

There was no time then to hunt around for things you might need. You had already dressed warmly. Ideally you had 'silk' at the neck, wrists and ankles which was one of the best ways to keep the body warm. You wore overalls or 'battle dress', high fur-lined flying boots with appropriate maps stuck into them, the mandatory helmet, microphone, oxygen mask, goggles, some first aid and then—if you wished—this interesting little plastic box stored in a deep pocket.

Combing through the dull coloured fragments, we all tried to figure out just what was inside. What appeared as dust was actually the remains of Bovril chocolate—a British concentrated high energy food bar. No argument with that; we often carried them anyway. Next a good sized compact plastic collapsible pouch with a snap enclosure—obviously for water when you find it. One can survive for quite a long time without food, but without water you are in jeopardy very quickly. I asked my gang, whose faces were now within inches of the table what they thought would be vital. The first answer was obvious; a compass. Right on! And here it was sealed in a tiny container, like a miniature restaurant package. Although its magnetic needle seemed to be easily affected by the metal on the table, it still worked.

The thoughtful authorities did not wish us to go hungry. Chocolate was maybe alright as a snack, but we needed a good meal it seemed, for *behold* the next item: a set of (now almost decomposed) fish hooks, a lure and a short fishing line. A comforting thought to imagine ourselves, feet dangling in the water, sitting on the bank of a French river or Dutch canal with our little fishing pole and cheerily flipping our catches out one by one onto the grass beside us.

Fish was clearly meant to be the first course only, for the military wildlife experts had come up with another winner: the title on the paper wrapper read *rabbit-snare instructions*. Here was the ultimate in forethought. Just find a clearly defined rabbit run and proceed as follows, it helpfully advised. We used to imagine ourselves ignoring the patrols, lights, dogs, German bayonets and other inconveniences with our faces to the wet turf carefully picking out a really smashing and well-travelled rodent highway. Here we would spread our noose, bend our willow twig, notch it neatly—you didn't by the way drop your parachute release knife when you bailed out, did you? We would set the tripwire, hold our breaths and wait. Come the dawn *presto* a fat rabbit, strangled, immobile and ready for the pot. Life was obviously looking up for the impromptu but unwilling tourist. A fire would be needed, but don't worry about damp wood because even though there are three packets of waterproof matches provided, we also have a container of fire making tablets and a powerful magnifying glass—possibly this is also to help read the small print in the dark on how to catch a fish. Knife a bit blunt? Still not to worry, there is a little steel sharpener tucked away in the corner of the box.

Well rested and well fed, it must be remembered that the fugitive—perhaps lying in a ditch somewhere—might wish to appear spic and span. More thoughtfulness; here is, yes, a piece of soap and not one, not two or even three, but no less than SIX razor blades. I could stay here looking sharp for a week. Digging still deeper, it is clear that the experts have anticipated every emergency, for suppose I am unfortunate enough to have a *really* bristly chin; the next treasures are two extra strong 'Star' razor blades, stamped in unmistakable type 'For Tough Beards'. In case of capture—to leave no doubt in the minds of a suspicious enemy—a conscientious manufacturer has seen to it that each blade is emblazoned in blue 'British Made'.

Incidentally such an oversight was no joke: a navigator friend of mine, hiding out after the capture of Crete by the Germans in 1941, watched in horror as the farmer who had been sheltering him, together with his wife and two children, were all shot in front of his eyes as he peered out from a trench in a covered foxhole below a haystack. An unexpected Nazi patrol had come by and saw a light blue shirt on the clothesline—a truly terrible lapse of judgement. It had just that same telltale UK label on the collar.

There are still a few pieces, down on the bottommost layer. It must mean it is time to contact our friends who may be overhead and wondering how the rabbit stew and fish chowder are lasting out. Possibly a large notice using this wax crayon? No, not too practical, but we have two better alternatives. First, a heliograph, an excellent device to signal aloft by means of a polished piece of metal, with a small sighting hole, especially effective in the Sahara Desert; and secondly, we had a spare flashlight bulb. What else could *possibly* be needed...? except perhaps... a flashlight...

So there it was, all spread out on the cottage table. We decided, for some sentimental reason, to put the crumbling kit back into its little plastic home. We sprinkled a little Bovril dust into the corners, sealed it up and stowed it away—perhaps for another three or four decades, by which time no one will have the faintest idea what it is and won't care either.

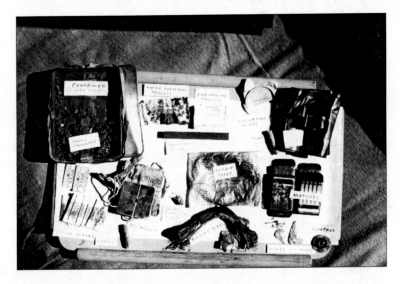

Our official Escape Kit, carried by pilots over Europe

22.

Wartime Spitfire Base Revisited

1988

I kept telling myself that the memory plays tricks on us. Yet all of a sudden there it was, the little windswept twelve-room hotel surrounded by a desultory huddle of grey, nondescript houses. It looked to me just the same. It stood hard against a severe granite church at the foot of a rugged headland on one of the most northerly tips of Scotland.

My mini car clipped through the empty-looking village of Castletown, round the wide arc of a sandy bay, on the dune side of a mile long deserted beach. I parked in the empty lot, paused for a long moment and then pushed open the door of the glass-fronted vestibule.

"And may I ask why you specially want that back room?" asked the rather dour middle-aged clerk.

"Oh, just a bit of nostalgia," I replied.

I followed her down the corridor, and she opened the last door with a large key and switched on the light. There were two beds, a chest, a wardrobe, a small table and a hard-backed chair.

"It's not the best," she said apologetically. She was right; the outlook was a blank wall, but I had decided to gladly pay for a night in that particular room. Forty years had passed since I'd been stationed at this desolate northern peninsula of the British Isles. I had slept in that left bed for quite some time. In the adjoining one had been 'Timber' Woods, the tall ex-Mountie who had joined the RAF to become a Spitfire pilot in 1940.

Our new squadron had taken over this small Inn as its home in the early part of our existence. We were a mixed bag of new, young flyers, British, Canadian, New Zealand, Polish, French and a Czech. Our average age was about twenty-one, except for the two flight commanders who had survived their first operational tour unscathed and, of course, our CO, who was an old man of twenty-seven.

The Royal Air Force, at this time, was forming defensive combat squadrons as fast as it could build fighter planes and train the pilots. The bombers were coming along but much more slowly due to priorities. My brother, five years my senior, started as a navigator and already had been frustrated with five doses of home leave to my one. A year later he would be killed when his plane was shot down on the return trip from Cologne in Nazi Germany.

Our primary job in the north was to meet and then patrol protection for the allied convoys, near the end of their Atlantic run, from the threat of Norway-based Focke-Wulf Condors.

Some convoys would limp in with a third of their ships already sent to the bottom by U-boats. We had to keep strict radio silence, and we sometimes wondered if we were protecting the right convoy, all of which zigzagged like mad, for obvious reasons.

After a pub lunch, I drove two miles over to the old base, hardly daring to expect that much of it would remain. To my amazement, and with the help of a bit of imagination, it was quite recognizable—almost frozen in time. It was strange, for there was no graffiti and little sign of vandalism, just steady decay.

Sheep were grazing on the barely discernible runways. A few buildings of the cluster of Station Headquarters were being used to store farm equipment, and several of the crew huts were dispersed along the perimeter with piles of manure outside and gaping holes where the windows had once kept out most of the cold.

The Y-shaped bomb-bay of earth and stone, where my aircraft had stood, was still there. It too was recognizable though collapsed on one side almost to ground level.

I wandered slowly into 'B' flight, to the alarm of exiting pigeons, and saw the crew room where my metal bed frame had claimed a spot beside the pot-bellied stove.

My imagination was starting to work overtime. Just a few feet away, on the far wall, Sgt. Middleton would be playing darts. Mike was winding up the old 78 rpm gramophone with its stock of Bakelite records—*Amapola* was the top hit—and tall Larché, from Mauritius, was regaling us with his jokes in broken English. Meanwhile Hornby, the only married one in our bunch, kept asking himself—and us—just why he'd voluntarily left his wife and landed himself in this crazy life.

There were two wires protruding from the plaster where the telephone operator had patiently sat, connected to Sector Control by land line.

Here we'd waited for the 'scramble' call that would send the first section into the air—funny how that tight feeling inside us would vanish when we were off and running for the waiting planes. Woe betide us later if we were not talking to base at Angels 10—10,000 feet—within three minutes of that terse message.

My mind flashed back to those World War II days. There was the main gate with the flag pole, guard house, whitewashed stones, and military police with blancoed belts and armbands. The hangars were a hive of activity with Spitfires in various stages of repair and maintenance, NAFFI wagons dishing out cups of char—tasting too often of carbolic soap—vans scuttling round the taxi track, bringing fresh pilots from the mess and removing sleepy ones.

It was here finally that the long-awaited message came, informing the squadron that it was moving to Biggin Hill, just south of London's bomb alley. *Biggin Hill*, the most famous of all fighter bases, with a tally of more than 1,000 enemies destroyed. We were ecstatic; this was it. It was from this base that we'd flown proudly south in beautiful formation through a fall mist.

For the next few months there was to be more order, more discipline, less laughter; casualties mounted. Half of the squadron was sent to the defence of Malta; a posting from which few of them ever returned.

As the sheep grazed contentedly around me, and I realized with a bit of a shock that I was probably one of only two or three who survived from that original little band of flyers. I had checked the names carved on the stone of the Runnymede Air Force's Memorial, a few miles outside Central London, looking for names I remembered. So many had been really fine young men. I can vividly recall their faces and the closeness of their friendship. Perhaps being wounded and spending a year on my back had some advantages; I had plenty of time to appreciate how fortunate I had been to survive the incredible incident that had taken me out of the war for a time.

I still have a crystal clear memory of diving out of control towards my point of impact.

My escape was a bit of a freak. A mid-air collision, anywhere, in cloud (high or low) was usually a recipe for not making it home. Thus I was not a high priority. However I was told afterwards that local anti-aircraft gunners had carried me off by ambulance to a local civilian facility. From there, some hours later the RAF took over and shuttled me to their central hospital in northwest London.

I had multiple injuries but apparently the message got a bit mixed up and I was marked as having a broken leg. The transportation over bombed out roads was a somewhat rough ride...

Remarkably the other pilot also survived; he pancaked onto the forward airfield to which we were trying to make emergency landings. His survival sadly did not last long; he was shot down and killed a short while later by a German FW 190 on an operation over northern France.

At the old airbase, it was quiet and peaceful, so I continued to sit outside with my back against a lump of concrete and let my mind drift...

While recuperating from injuries, I had been able to wander around a few of the devastated areas where my family had had roots. No wonder the British, epitomized by defiant Winston Churchill, were proud of their stubbornness, insane cheerfulness, and their stoic determination.

I thought back to where my grandfather's office had stood, right beside Manchester Cathedral—actually it was known as No.1 Cathedral St. The building was destroyed in 1940 by a land-mine. It simply disappeared, leaving a huge hole in the rubble. The very large safe that housed the main records and had stood in the corner by the window also vanished, never to be seen again. The other business office was in nearby Liverpool, the busiest port then in England and likewise very heavily bombed. It was in the imposing ten-storey India Building which was burned to a shell.

The manager of our business, a man named Wilson, whether as a night raid casualty or as a result of a heart attack, died. I remember visiting his Spanish born widow to pay my respects. There he was laid out stone dead on his dining room table. It was an import/export business, and I was appointed a director of the moribund company, in order to represent the family's interests. I was young and knew next to zero about the whole matter. For years I had an economic albatross around my neck in the shape of a warehouse full of electric motors that nobody wanted or could ship out. I just could not get rid of them. For years I kept dreaming about those pesky crates.

Still then on that windy, Northern coast my mind travelled further and further afield to World War I, the war that was to end all wars, the war that took twenty million lives—so I was told when I was at school. A mere twenty-one years later the world fell again into war. By then the world managed to slaughter forty million human beings. Mass aerial bombing this time included women and children; instead of trench warfare there were thousands of tanks, hundreds of U-boats, countless aircraft, with new weapons such as V1s that could take out a whole suburban block at a time. Later came the V2s, the first highly successful—but too late in the war—stratospheric rockets developed by the Germans with devastating high-explosive effect. Travelling by bus near Hyde Park in London one day, but for a brief traffic delay, I might have been vaporized by one of them. The hotel that I would probably have just been passing two minutes later had a direct hit and, literally vanished from existence.

Our strange political history has changed little since the dawn of time. Our recent enemies when hostilities ended soon became our greatest allies. Japan teaches us cogent lessons still about discipline, sacrifice, obedience, even some strong patriotism. Germany the other war 'loser' was slowly becoming the strongest economically, the most populous and probably the most prosperous country in Europe. To think that by 1945 Germany had suffered such widespread devastation, whole cities wiped out, far worse even than what was suffered by England, and yet today there is often hardly a trace of it all, so much rebuilt and almost better—Poland too, even Russia. The carnage fades from most of the history books. Millions of young people today have barely any close knowledge of World War II.

The World is still very much troubled but also very much travelled; whole populations migrate to support their families elsewhere. I think of folk that I meet and listen to their memories; soldiers who took part in the 900 day siege of Leningrad, very elderly survivors of the horrors of the Nazi concentration camps. I reflect on my visit to Auschwitz in Poland, the acme of barbarism and cruelty beyond mankind's worst imagination of depravity. One of my wife's close friends was in the Red Cross, part of the first team to enter Belsen. The sight of mountains of rotting corpses was enough to turn her mind so that she never recovered.

Now, in contrast, some of my blood relations are lovely young Germans living near the town of Munich, scene of Hitler's huge Nazi rallies. And I thought to myself, as I sat at the edge of our once vibrant base, it is far too easy to ruminate on violence, death and destruction; the press ensures we never cease to focus upon them. Yet the opposite exists. Love and compassion are everywhere.

My mind slips back to the scudding clouds above me and the sheep and the waving grass and the murmur of the sea over the dunes in the distance. The sheer goodness one finds in nearly all human beings, in old friends, in former enemies—what an obscene word—in strangers we meet everywhere... is staggering.

We are all related and interrelated. You have but to spend some time alone with someone, provided there is mutual desire for communication, to learn that they have a story. We are all sentient beings, our real needs are basically the same. Despite all our deficiencies, we still have a wonderful world.

I got up, shivered a bit, and wrapped my long scarf tighter around my neck. It was time to go. Yet solemn, forlorn thoughts persisted emphasized by the distant call of strident seabirds.

I have always felt in hindsight that being a casualty was an enriching experience. It helped to give my life a focus, a direction and a purpose. Stretching over six years of war, I have a kaleidoscope of memories, and like so many other aircrew, I am amazed that I survived the multitude of times that my demise was millimetres away. That doesn't sound like a very heroic achievement, but I do keep recognizing that I was not one of the fifty-two pilots of our squadron who failed to make it to the end of hostilities.

So there I stood, all those years later, rather foolishly taking pictures of a flat brown landscape, dotted with the crumbling remains of a few empty buildings. *Was it really only two generations ago?*

Squadron Mess NE Scotland

**RAF Fighter Groups
(1940)**

ABOUT THE AUTHOR

Richard Gilman was born in Vancouver, B.C. in 1922. During World War II he spent six years in the Royal Air Force. While he insists his service, compared with so many others, was quite unspectacular, he did manage to crash four times including a mid-air collision while returning from an operation off the coast of Nazi-held France.

After the War, Richard obtained an M.A. at Oxford and began a fascinating 40 year career in education (on four continents). He has been an enthusiastic community volunteer, travelling widely, leading student tour groups, delivering cargo for refugees in South East Asia, surveying school sites for development in tropical Africa, teaching in Central Europe and the Republic of China, promoting the cause of disarmament and world peace – and, for fun, skydiving on his 80th birthday – this time with a parachute!

Before he retired, he was awarded the Queen's Jubilee Medal for Service to Canadian Education.

Richard and Kay – a talented artist – had four children, each qualified in a different profession. Richard is a proud Grandfather to eleven grandchildren and a growing clan of 'greats'. In 1992, he married Retha, a mother of five and a gifted administrator.

Richard now lives in Qualicum Beach on picturesque Vancouver Island.

CPSIA information can be obtained at www.ICGtesting.com
Printed in the USA
LVOW08s0023250314

378711LV00008B/795/P